THE GOSPEL CALL
AND TRUE
CONVERSION

Recovering the Gospel

The Gospel's Power and Message

The Gospel Call and True Conversion

Gospel Assurance and Warnings

THE GOSPEL CALL
AND TRUE
CONVERSION

PAUL WASHER

Reformation Heritage Books
Grand Rapids, Michigan

The Gospel Call and True Conversion
© 2013 Paul Washer

Reformation Heritage Books
3070 29th St. SE
Grand Rapids, MI 49512
616-977-0889
e-mail: orders@heritagebooks.org
website: www.heritagebooks.org

Printed in the United States of America
22 23 24 25 26/12 11 10 9 8 7 6

Scripture taken from the New King James Version®. Copyright © 1982 by Thomas Nelson, Inc. Used by permission. All rights reserved.

Library of Congress Cataloging-in-Publication Data

Washer, Paul, 1961-
 The gospel call and true conversion / Paul Washer.
   pages cm. — (Recovering the gospel)
 Includes bibliographical references.
 ISBN 978-1-60178-236-6 (pbk. : alk. paper) 1. Conversion—Christianity. I. Title.
 BV4916.3.W37 2013
 248.2′4—dc23
                    2013011095

For additional Reformed literature, request a free book list from Reformation Heritage Books at the above address.

Contents

Series Preface: Recovering the Gospel

The gospel of Jesus Christ is the greatest of all treasures given to the church and the individual Christian. It is not *a* message among many but *the* message above them all. It is the power of God for salvation and the greatest revelation of the manifold wisdom of God to men and angels.[1] It is for this reason that the apostle Paul gave the gospel the first place in his preaching, endeavored with all his might to proclaim it clearly, and even pronounced a curse upon all those who would pervert its truth.[2]

Each generation of Christians is a steward of the gospel message, and through the power of the Holy Spirit, God calls upon us to guard this treasure that has been entrusted to us.[3] If we are to be faithful stewards, we must be absorbed in the study of the gospel, take great pains to understand its truths, and pledge ourselves to guard its contents.[4] In doing so, we will ensure salvation both for ourselves and for those who hear us.[5]

This stewardship drives me to write these books. I have little desire for the hard work of writing, and there is certainly no lack of Christian books, but I have put the following collection of sermons in written form for the same reason that I preached them: to be free from their burden. Like Jeremiah, if I do not speak forth this message, "then…in my heart [it becomes] like a burning fire shut up in my bones; and I was weary of holding it back, and I could not."[6] As the apostle Paul exclaimed, "Woe is me if I do not preach the gospel!"[7]

---

1. Romans 1:16; Ephesians 3:10
2. 1 Corinthians 15:3; Colossians 4:4; Galatians 1:8–9
3. 2 Timothy 1:14
4. 1 Timothy 4:15
5. 1 Timothy 4:16
6. Jeremiah 20:9
7. 1 Corinthians 9:16

As is commonly known, the word *gospel* comes from the Greek word *euangélion*, which is properly translated "good news." In one sense, every page of Scripture contains the gospel, but in another sense, the gospel refers to a very specific message—the salvation accomplished for a fallen people through the life, death, resurrection, and ascension of Jesus Christ, the Son of God.

In accordance with the Father's good pleasure, the eternal Son, who is equal with the Father and is the exact representation of His nature, willingly left the glory of heaven, was conceived by the Holy Spirit in the womb of a virgin, and was born the God-man: Jesus of Nazareth.[8] As a man, He walked on this earth in perfect obedience to the law of God.[9] In the fullness of time, men rejected and crucified Him. On the cross, He bore man's sin, suffered God's wrath, and died in man's place.[10] On the third day, God raised Him from the dead. This resurrection is the divine declaration that the Father has accepted His Son's death as a sacrifice for sin. Jesus paid the penalty for man's disobedience, satisfied the demands of justice, and appeased the wrath of God.[11] Forty days after the resurrection, the Son of God ascended into the heavens, sat down at the right hand of the Father, and was given glory, honor, and dominion over all.[12] There, in the presence of God, He represents His people and makes requests to God on their behalf.[13] All who acknowledge their sinful, helpless state and throw themselves upon Christ, God will fully pardon, declare righteous, and reconcile unto Himself.[14] This is the gospel of God and of Jesus Christ, His Son.

One of the greatest crimes committed by this present Christian generation is its neglect of the gospel, and it is from this neglect that all our other maladies spring forth. The lost world is not so much gospel hardened as it is gospel ignorant because many of those who proclaim the gospel are also ignorant of its most basic truths. The essential themes that make up the very core of the gospel—the justice of God, the radical depravity of man, the blood atonement, the nature of true conversion,

---

8. Acts 2:23; Hebrews 1:3; Philippians 2:6–7; Luke 1:35
9. Hebrews 4:15
10. 1 Peter 2:24; 3:18; Isaiah 53:10
11. Luke 24:6; Romans 1:4; Romans 4:25
12. Hebrews 1:3; Matthew 28:18; Daniel 7:13–14
13. Luke 24:51; Philippians 2:9–11; Hebrews 1:3; Hebrews 7:25
14. Mark 1:15; Romans 10:9; Philippians 3:3

and the biblical basis of assurance—are absent from too many pulpits. Churches reduce the gospel message to a few creedal statements, teach that conversion is a mere human decision, and pronounce assurance of salvation over anyone who prays the sinner's prayer.

The result of this gospel reductionism has been far-reaching. First, it further hardens the hearts of the unconverted. Few modern-day "converts" ever make their way into the fellowship of the church, and those who do often fall away or have lives marked by habitual carnality. Untold millions walk our streets and sit in our pews unchanged by the true gospel of Jesus Christ, and yet they are convinced of their salvation because one time in their life they raised a hand at an evangelistic campaign or repeated a prayer. This false sense of security creates a great barrier that often insulates such individuals from ever hearing the true gospel.

Secondly, such a gospel deforms the church from a spiritual body of regenerated believers into a gathering of carnal men who profess to know God, but by their deeds they deny Him.[15] With the preaching of the true gospel, men come to the church without gospel entertainment, special activities, or the promise of benefits beyond those offered by the gospel. Those who come do so because they desire Christ and are hungry for biblical truth, heartfelt worship, and opportunities for service. When the church proclaims a lesser gospel, it fills up with carnal men who share little interest in the things of God, and the maintenance of such men is a heavy burden upon the church.[16] The church then tones down the radical demands of the gospel to a convenient morality, and true devotion to Christ gives way to activities designed to meet the felt needs of its members. The church becomes activity-driven rather than Christ-centered, and it carefully filters or repackages the truth so as not to offend the carnal majority. The church lays aside the great truths of Scripture and orthodox Christianity, and pragmatism (i.e., whatever keeps the church going and growing) becomes the rule of the day.

Thirdly, such a gospel reduces evangelism and missions to little more than a humanistic endeavor driven by clever marketing strategies based upon a careful study of the latest trends in culture. After years of witnessing the impotence of an unbiblical gospel, many evangelicals seem convinced that the gospel will not work and that man has somehow

---

15. Titus 1:16
16. 1 Corinthians 2:14

become too complex a being to be saved and transformed by such a simple and scandalous message. There is now more emphasis on understanding our fallen culture and its fads than on understanding and proclaiming the only message that has the power to save it. As a result, the gospel is constantly being repackaged to fit what contemporary culture deems most relevant. We have forgotten that the true gospel is always relevant to every culture because it is God's eternal word to every man.

Fourthly, such a gospel brings reproach to the name of God. Through the proclamation of a lesser gospel, the carnal and unconverted come into the fellowship of the church, and through the almost total neglect of biblical church discipline, they are allowed to stay without correction or reproof. This soils the purity and reputation of the church and blasphemes the name of God among the unbelieving.[17] In the end, God is not glorified, the church is not edified, the unconverted church member is not saved, and the church has little or no witness to the unbelieving world.

It does not become us as ministers or laymen to stand so near and do nothing when we see "the glorious gospel of our blessed God" replaced by a gospel of lesser glory.[18] As stewards of this trust, we have a duty to recover the one true gospel and proclaim it boldly and clearly to all. We would do well to pay heed to the words of Charles Haddon Spurgeon:

> In these days, I feel bound to go over the elementary truths of the gospel repeatedly. In peaceful times, we may feel free to make excursions into interesting districts of truth which lie far afield; but now we must stay at home, and guard the hearts and homes of the church by defending the first principles of the faith. In this age, there have risen up in the church itself men who speak perverse things. There be many that trouble us with their philosophies and novel interpretations, whereby they deny the doctrines they profess to teach, and undermine the faith they are pledged to maintain. It is well that some of us, who know what we believe, and have no secret meanings for our words, should just put our foot down and maintain our standing, holding forth the word of life, and plainly declaring the foundation truths of the gospel of Jesus Christ.[19]

---

17. Romans 2:24

18. 1 Timothy 1:11

19. Charles H. Spurgeon, *The Metropolitan Tabernacle Pulpit* (repr., Pasadena, Tex.: Pilgrim Publications), 32:385.

Although the Recovering the Gospel series does not represent an entirely systematic presentation of the gospel, it does address most of the essential elements, especially those that are most neglected in contemporary Christianity. It is my hope that these words might be a guide to help you rediscover the gospel in all its beauty, scandal, and saving power. It is my prayer that such a rediscovery might transform your life, strengthen your proclamation, and bring the greatest glory to God.

Your brother,
Paul David Washer

PART ONE
The Gospel Call

Jesus came to Galilee, preaching the gospel of the kingdom of God, and saying, "The time is fulfilled, and the kingdom of God is at hand. Repent, and believe in the gospel."
—Mark 1:14–15

I kept back nothing that was helpful, but proclaimed it to you, and taught you publicly and from house to house, testifying to Jews, and also to Greeks, repentance toward God and faith toward our Lord Jesus Christ.
—Acts 20:20–21

But what does it say? "The word is near you, in your mouth and in your heart" (that is, the word of faith which we preach): that if you confess with your mouth the Lord Jesus and believe in your heart that God has raised Him from the dead, you will be saved. For with the heart one believes unto righteousness, and with the mouth confession is made unto salvation.
—Romans 10:8–10

CHAPTER ONE

A Call to Repentance

Jesus came to Galilee, preaching the gospel of the kingdom of God, and saying, "The time is fulfilled, and the kingdom of God is at hand. Repent, and believe in the gospel."

—Mark 1:14–15

Truly, these times of ignorance God overlooked, but now commands all men everywhere to repent.

—Acts 17:30

According to God's eternal plan and good pleasure, the Son of God, equal with the Father and the exact representation of His nature, willingly left the glory of heaven, was conceived by the Holy Spirit in the womb of a virgin, and was born the God-man. He walked on this earth in perfect obedience to the law of God, and then, in the fullness of time, He was rejected by men and crucified. On the cross, He carried the sins of His people, was forsaken of God, suffered divine wrath, and died condemned. On the third day, God raised Him from the dead as a public declaration that His death was accepted, the punishment for sin was paid, the demands of justice were satisfied, and the wrath of God was appeased. Forty days after the resurrection, Jesus Christ, the Son of God and Son of Man, ascended to heaven, where He sat down at the right hand of God the Father and was given glory, honor, and dominion over all. There, in the presence of God, He represents His people and makes requests and special petitions to God on their behalf. This is the good news of God and of Jesus Christ, His Son.[1]

Having considered this great thing that God has done, we must now turn our attention toward humanity. What is a person's biblical response

---

1. This summary is based in part on Westminster Confession, chapter 8.

to the gospel? How should the evangelist direct desperate people when they cry, "What must I do to be saved?" The Scriptures are clear: people must repent and believe the gospel. When Jesus appeared to Israel, He did not plead with them to open their hearts and ask Him in, nor did He direct them to repeat a certain prayer. Instead, He commanded them to turn from their sin and believe the gospel.[2]

AN ENDURING AND UNCHANGING CALL

Before we continue on, we must understand that Christ's command of repentance and faith is still applicable for us today. It would be terribly wrong to think that it was limited to a certain dispensation or directed only to the Jews of the New Testament era. "Repent and believe!" is the gospel call for yesterday, today, and forever. The apostles reinforced this truth and boldly proclaimed it after Christ's resurrection and ascension. Note the apostle Paul's declarations:

> I kept back nothing that was helpful, but proclaimed it to you, and taught you publicly and from house to house, testifying to Jews, and also to Greeks, repentance toward God and faith toward our Lord Jesus Christ (Acts 20:20–21).

> Truly, these times of ignorance God overlooked, but now commands all men everywhere to repent (Acts 17:30).

These texts and several others prove that there is no ground for any argument that would relegate repentance to some earlier dispensation or diminish its part in modern-day evangelistic preaching. "Repentance unto God" was the call of the Old Testament prophets, John the Baptist, the Lord Jesus Christ, the apostles, and the confessions and preaching of the most pious and useful theologians, preachers, and missionaries throughout the history of the church. The Westminster and New Hampshire Confessions state respectively:

> Repentance unto life is an evangelical grace; the doctrine thereof is to be preached by every minister of the Gospel, as well as that of faith in Christ (15.1).

> We believe that repentance and faith are sacred duties, and also inseparable graces (art. 8).

---

2. See Mark 1:14–15 for one example.

THE ESSENTIAL CHARACTERISTICS OF GENUINE REPENTANCE

Since the call to repentance is an absolute necessity in the proclamation of the gospel, we need to have a right understanding of the nature of repentance and its manifestation in genuine conversion. The following are eight essential characteristics of true biblical repentance:

- change of mind
- sorrow for sin
- personal acknowledgment and confession of sin
- turning away from sin
- renunciation of self-righteousness or good works
- turning to God
- practical obedience
- continuing and deepening work of repentance

It is imperative for us to understand that these characteristics of genuine repentance will not necessarily appear in their fullest or most mature form at the moment of conversion but will continue to grow and deepen throughout the believer's life. It would be terribly misleading and destructive to suggest that true conversion requires that a person should attain a depth of repentance and faith that is rarely seen in the life of the most mature Christian. Jesus Himself said that even the faith of a mustard seed is sufficient to move mountains if it is genuine.[3] At the time of conversion, a person's grasp of the heinous nature of sin may be meager, but it will be real. The depth of a new convert's brokenness may be slight compared to that of the mature believer, but it will most certainly be genuine. The final evidence that a person's repentance and faith are unto salvation will be that both these graces will continue to grow and deepen in his or her life through God's enduring work of sanctification. With these clarifications and cautions in mind, let's take a closer look at each of these characteristics.

Change of Mind

In the New Testament, the word *repent* is most frequently translated from a Greek verb that is constructed from another verb that means "to perceive or understand" and a preposition that denotes change.[4] Repentance,

---

3. Matthew 17:20

4. *Metanoéo.*"The preposition *meta* used with verbs of motion and of mental activity indicates a change in the meaning of the simple verb." *New International Dictionary of New Testament Theology,* ed. Colin Brown (Grand Rapids: Zondervan, 1975), 1:357.

therefore, involves a radical change in a person's perception of things or in his view of reality. In the Scriptures, this change of mind is never confined to the intellect but has an equally radical effect on the emotions and will. In summary, genuine repentance begins with a work of the Holy Spirit in the life of the sinner, whereby He regenerates the heart, illumines the mind, and exposes error by a revelation of divine truth. Because of this divine work, the sinner's mind is changed and his view of reality is radically altered—especially with regard to God, self, sin, and the way of salvation.

The Scriptures teach that prior to conversion, a man is darkened in his understanding and walks in the futility of his mind.[5] Furthermore, his mind is hostile toward God, suppresses the truth of God, and cannot subject itself to the law of God.[6] Consequently, the unconverted person has a completely distorted view of reality, and it is not an exaggeration to say that he is wrong about everything that truly matters. He knows something of the one true God and His majesty, but he does not think it necessary to honor Him as God or give thanks.[7] He is filled with self and sees the promotion of self as the end of all things. The laws of God are written on his heart, but he does not think it necessary or advantageous to follow their dictates. Instead, he fights against his conscience and seeks to suppress what he knows to be true.[8] He knows that all who commit evil deeds are worthy of death, but he does not think it necessary to fear. He not only does the same things but also gives hearty approval to those who practice them.[9] His own mortality confronts him as death swallows up everyone around him, but he does not think the plague will ever reach his doorstep. To put it simply, the unconverted person is wrong and yet arrogantly continues to do what is right in his own eyes.[10] He is on a way that seems right to him, but its end is the way of death.[11]

However, at the moment of conversion, the Spirit of God regenerates a person's heart, and the truth enlightens his darkened mind. Then, as a blind man given sight or a sleeper awakened from a dream, he is made

5. Ephesians 4:17–18
6. Romans 1:18; 8:7
7. Romans 1:21
8. Romans 2:14–15
9. Romans 1:32
10. Judges 17:6; 21:25
11. Proverbs 14:12

aware that his entire life has been governed by his own delusions and that he has been wrong about everything. For the first time in his life, he sees and acknowledges what is true. His wrong and even blasphemous thoughts about God are replaced by a meager yet accurate understanding of the one true God. His vain opinions of his own virtue and merit are replaced by an awareness of the depravity of his nature and the utter wretchedness of his deeds. His arrogance, self-confidence, and independence are replaced by genuine humility, mistrust of self, brokenness over sin, and dependence upon God, to whom he looks for pardon. He then casts himself upon the mercies of God in the person and work of Jesus Christ and sets himself to doing the will of God. Thus, his mind has been changed and his life transformed. He has repented.

Saul of Tarsus is a great example of biblical repentance. In his ignorance and unbelief, he saw Jesus of Nazareth as nothing more than an impostor and a blasphemer, and he thought that all who followed Him were worthy of imprisonment and death.[12] Thus, he went to the high priest, "breathing threats and murder against the disciples of the Lord," and asked for letters so that "if he found any who were of the Way, whether men or women, he might bring them bound to Jerusalem" (Acts 9:2–3). Yet on Saul's way to Damascus, the glorified Christ confronted him.[13] At that moment, Saul's entire view of reality disintegrated. He discovered that he had been wrong about everything. He had thought that Jesus of Nazareth was a blasphemer, only to discover that He was the Son of God, the promised Messiah, and the Savior of the world. He had thought that righteousness was earned through obedience to the law, only to discover that there was nothing good in him and that salvation was by grace through faith and not of oneself, but a gift of God.[14] He had thought that the disciples were the enemies of Israel and unfit to live, only to discover that he was persecuting the true Israel and putting to death the sons and daughters of the living God.[15] Thus, he sat alone for three days "without sight, and neither ate nor drank" (Acts 9:9). Through one encounter with the truth that is Christ Jesus, Saul of Tarsus, the proud and self-righteous Pharisee of Pharisees, was broken into a million pieces. Yet,

12. Acts 9:1–2; 1 Timothy 1:13
13. Acts 9:3–8
14. Romans 7:18; Ephesians 2:8–9
15. Acts 8:1; Romans 8:14–15; Galatians 6:16

through the illuminating and regenerating work of the Holy Spirit, his heart and mind were changed, and his life was radically altered forever. He repented, got up, and was baptized; he took food and was strengthened. Then he immediately began to proclaim Jesus in the synagogues, saying, "He is the Son of God" (Acts 9:18–22). The news spread throughout all the churches of Judea that "'He who formerly persecuted us now preaches the faith which he once tried to destroy'" (Galatians 1:22–23).

Paul describes this radical reversal of his life that began on the road to Damascus in the following words. In them, we discover the power of a mind changed and a heart renewed by the regenerating work of the Holy Spirit:

> But what things were gain to me, these I have counted loss for Christ. Yet indeed I also count all things loss for the excellence of the knowledge of Christ Jesus my Lord, for whom I have suffered the loss of all things, and count them as rubbish, that I may gain Christ and be found in Him, not having my own righteousness, which is from the law, but that which is through faith in Christ, the righteousness which is from God by faith (Phil. 3:7–9).

Sorrow for Sin

A Hebrew term that adds to our understanding of *repentance* is the verb *nacham*. It is derived from a root that reflects the idea of "'breathing deeply,' communicating the physical display of one's feelings, such as sorrow, regret, or contrition."[16] Thus, biblical repentance not only involves a change of mind but also a genuine sorrow for sin.

The slightest true comprehension of our sinfulness and guilt will lead to genuine sorrow, shame, and even a healthy hatred or loathing of our sin and ourselves. Ezra the scribe declared that he was "ashamed and humiliated" to lift up his face to God because of Israel's sins (9:5–6). The prophet Jeremiah cried out, "We lie down in our shame, and our reproach covers us. For we have sinned against the LORD our God, we and our fathers, from our youth even to this day, and have not obeyed the voice of the LORD our God" (Jer. 3:25). The prophet Ezekiel was even so bold to declare that when disobedient Israel finally recognized the heinous nature of its sin against the Lord, it would loathe itself in its own

---

16. R. Laird Harris, Gleason L. Archer Jr., and Bruce K. Waltke, *Theological Workbook of the Old Testament* (Chicago: Moody Press, 1980), 2:570.

sight for all the evil things it had done.[17] Finally, writing to the believers in Rome, the apostle Paul noted that they were still ashamed of the things they had done prior to their conversion.[18]

Such talk seems out of place in a world and evangelical community overrun with the psychology of self-esteem, but sorrow, shame, and self-hatred are biblical truths and an essential part of genuine repentance in both the Old and New Testaments. These teachings of the Lord Jesus Christ and the apostle Paul give clear evidence of this truth:

> And the tax collector, standing afar off, would not so much as raise his eyes to heaven, but beat his breast, saying, "God, be merciful to me a sinner!"I tell you, this man went down to his house justified rather than the other; for everyone who exalts himself will be humbled, and he who humbles himself will be exalted (Luke 18:13–14).

> Now I rejoice, not that you were made sorry, but that your sorrow led to repentance. For you were made sorry in a godly manner, that you might suffer loss from us in nothing. For godly sorrow produces repentance leading to salvation, not to be regretted; but the sorrow of the world produces death (2 Cor. 7:9–10).

Faced with the reality of what he was and what he had done, the tax collector accompanied his confession with brokenness, deep remorse, and humility. In the case of the Corinthian church's carnality and pride, sorrow was not only appropriate but was also considered to be "according to the will of God." In both cases, however, it is important to notice that sorrow and shame were not the goal, but the means to a greater end. The publican's self-humiliation led to his justification, and the sorrow of the believers in Corinth led to repentance without regret, resulting in salvation.

Although there is a "sorrow of the world" that is without faith and leads to death as in the case of Judas Iscariot, we should never look negatively at the godly sorrow that accompanies genuine repentance and leads to life (2 Cor. 7:10). It is the testimony of Scripture that God highly esteems such sorrow. He will not despise "a broken and a contrite heart" (Ps. 51:17), but rather He looks to the one who is "poor and of a contrite spirit, and who trembles at My word" (Isa. 66:2). Though He dwells on a high and holy place, He is also with the contrite and lowly of spirit in

---

17. Ezekiel 20:43
18. Romans 6:21

order to revive them.[19] As Jesus taught us in the Beatitudes, "Blessed are those who mourn, for they shall be comforted" (Matt. 5:4).

Personal Acknowledgment and Confession of Sin

Repentance not only involves inward sorrow of the heart but also personal acknowledgment and open confession that God's opinion of us is true and His verdict is just: we are sinners, we have sinned, and we deserve divine condemnation. Biblical repentance always involves an owning up to what we are and what we have done. This truth runs contrary to the beliefs of our contemporary culture. We are a self-excusing and self-justifying people who, according to popular thought, are never truly at fault, but we are always victims of some malicious and often nameless power beyond our control. We find or invent the cleverest means of attributing our sins to anything or anyone outside of ourselves. We self-righteously point the finger at society, education, upbringing, or circumstance, and are appalled and even angered at the slightest indication that guilt should be laid at our feet. However, when we are converted, we have a radically altered understanding of this opinion of the age. For the first time in our lives, we turn our indicting finger back upon ourselves and honestly own up to our sin. Our mouths are shut, and we see ourselves as accountable to God.[20] We offer no excuse and seek no avenue of escape.

We accompany our personal acknowledgment of guilt—our taking full responsibility for our deeds—with an honest transparency before God and a heartfelt confession of sin. The word *confess* comes from a Greek word that literally means "to speak the same thing."[21] In the divine work of conversion, God opens up the heart of the sinner and speaks to him about his sin. The Word of God, living, active, and sharper than any two-edged sword, pierces the very depths of his heart and exposes even its deepest thoughts and intentions.[22] Then, for the first time in his life, the sinner comes face-to-face with his sin and understands something of its heinous nature. It is ever before him, and, try as he might, he cannot remove the horrid image of himself that he sees.[23] He can no longer hide but must acknowledge his sin before God and confess his transgressions

---

19. Isaiah 57:15
20. Romans 3:19
21. Greek: *homologéo*.
22. Hebrews 4:12
23. Psalm 51:3

to the Lord.[24] Like David, he is compelled to cry out in full recognition of
his guilt and in willing confession:

> Against You, You only, have I sinned,
> And done this evil in Your sight—
> That You may be found just when You speak,
> And blameless when You judge (Ps. 51:4).

The prophet Hosea describes the believer's new transparency before
God, by which he enters into agreement with Him and openly confesses
that everything God says about him is true:

> Take words with you,
> And return to the LORD.
> Say to Him,"Take away all iniquity;
> Receive us graciously,
> For we will offer the sacrifices of our lips" (14:2).

It is important to note that such sensitivity to sin and confession of it is
a mark of a true believer, but the lack of such is evidence that a person
may still be in an unconverted state. The apostle John writes, "If we say
that we have no sin, we deceive ourselves, and the truth is not in us [i.e.,
we are not Christian]. If we confess our sins, He is faithful and just to
forgive us our sins and to cleanse us from all unrighteousness [i.e., we are
Christian]. If we say that we have not sinned, we make Him a liar, and
His word is not in us [i.e., we are not Christian]" (1 John 1:8–10).

One of the greatest evidences of true conversion is not sinless perfection, as some have erroneously supposed. Instead, it is sensitivity to sin,
transparency before God regarding sin, and open confession of sin.

Turning Away from Sin

In the Old Testament, the word *repents* is translated primarily from a
Hebrew word that means "to return or turn back."[25] It implies not only a
turning away from evil, but also a turning to righteousness.[26] Therefore,
one of the telltale signs of genuine repentance will be honest and sincere
forsaking or turning away from sin. The abundance of tears a person may
shed or the apparent sincerity of his confession alone is never definite

---

24. Psalm 32:5
25. Hebrew: *shuwb.*
26. Harris, Archer, and Waltke, *Theological Workbook of the Old Testament,* 2:909.

evidence of biblical repentance. All this must be accompanied by a turning away from that which God hates and opposes. This truth is so clearly
set forth in the Scriptures that it requires very little commentary, as in
these three verses from the prophet Ezekiel:

> Thus says the Lord GOD: "Repent, turn away from your idols, and
> turn your faces away from all your abominations" (14:6).

> Repent, and turn from all your transgressions, so that iniquity will
> not be your ruin. Cast away from you all the transgressions which
> you have committed (18:30–31).

> "As I live," says the Lord GOD, "I have no pleasure in the death of
> the wicked, but that the wicked turn from his way and live. Turn,
> turn from your evil ways! For why should you die, O house of
> Israel?" (33:11).

It is an undeniable biblical truth that genuine repentance will
manifest itself in a turning away from sin. However, this truth about
repentance has often led to confusion and fear, among even the most
pious believers. Such confusion often manifests itself in the following
questions: Have I truly repented if I again commit the sin that I have
renounced and abhor? Do my frequent failures indicate that I am unrepentant? This very sensitive question requires a great deal of balance.
On the one hand, a frequent return to sin and lack of any sustained victory over it may be evidence of a superficial and unbiblical repentance.
This is why John the Baptist admonished the Pharisees to "bear fruits
worthy of repentance," and Jesus declared, "These people draw near to
Me with their mouth, and honor Me with their lips, but their heart is far
from Me" (Matt. 3:8; 15:7–8).

On the other hand, regardless of the progress a believer has made in
sanctification, even the most mature one will find the Christian life to
be a great struggle against sin with frequent battles, great victories, and
discouraging defeats. On this side of heaven, no believer will ever make
a complete break with sin to be immune from its deception and free
from all moral failure. Although true believers will grow in their forsaking of sin, sin will still be a repetitive malady in their lives. Although it
may become less frequent or pronounced, sin will never be eradicated
completely until the believer's ultimate glorification in heaven. Although
God has promised to cleanse us "from all [our] filthiness and from all
[our] idols," the most mature believer among us will at times be caught

in the very sin that he or she has renounced (Ezek. 36:25). Though we struggle against sin and run for holiness as one who runs for the prize; though we discipline our body and make it our slave; and though we walk in this world with the greatest care and wisdom, we will find that we are not yet perfected and still in need of repentance and grace.[27] For this reason, believers should not despair about the battle they wage or their frequent need of repentance as they struggle against sin. The reality of such a struggle is a mark of true conversion. The false convert—the hypocrite—knows no such battle. It is important to remember that God does not promise His presence to the one who is perfect, but to the one whose life is marked by a broken and contrite spirit and who trembles at His word.[28]

So, then, a great balance is required. There are two sides to this coin, and one cannot be lost without the other. On one hand, genuine Christians will experience a gradual progress in sanctification and frequent victories over sin. He who began a good work of repentance in them will continue that work so that it grows and deepens and becomes a greater and greater reality in their lives.[29] However, Christians will never be free from sin completely or without need of the divine gift of repentance. On the other hand, professing Christians who demonstrate no real progress in sanctification and who rarely bring forth fruit worthy of repentance should be greatly concerned for their souls. They should test and examine themselves to see if they are in the faith.[30]

Renunciation of Works
At first glance, this may seem to be an inappropriate characteristic of genuine repentance. After all, we believe we are "created in Christ Jesus for good works, which God prepared beforehand that we should walk in them" (Eph. 2:10). Furthermore, John the Baptist tells us to bear fruit or do works that are worthy of repentance, and James tells us that faith without works is dead.[31] How, then, is true repentance manifested by a renunciation of works? The answer is in Hebrews 6:1: "Therefore, leaving the discussion of the elementary principles of Christ, let us go on

---

27. 1 Corinthians 9:24–27; Ephesians 5:15
28. Isaiah 66:2
29. Philippians 1:6
30. 2 Corinthians 13:5
31. Matthew 3:8; Luke 3:8; James 2:17, 26

to perfection, not laying again the foundation of repentance from dead works and of faith toward God." The phrase "repentance from dead works" refers to a renouncing or turning away from any and every hope in some personal work of piety as a means of justification or right standing before God. Any work that a person might rely upon in place of the person and work of Christ is a dead work that cannot save.

Scripture teaches that salvation is by grace alone through faith alone; it is not of works, lest any man should boast.[32] This is why the Scriptures present grace and works as diametrically opposed to one another and mutually exclusive. The apostle Paul sets forth this truth brilliantly in his letter to the church at Rome: "And if [salvation is] by grace, then it is no longer of works; otherwise grace is no longer grace" (Rom. 11:6).

In classical logic there is a principle called the law of noncontradiction that states that contradictory statements cannot both be true at the same time and in the same context. This is true with regard to works and grace as they pertain to salvation. If salvation is by grace, it cannot be by works; if it is by works, it cannot be by grace. Therefore, before a person can exercise true saving faith in Christ, he must first abandon all hope of attaining salvation through any other means.

This abandonment of self-righteousness in favor of Christ alone is one of the great works of the Spirit of God in regeneration. Through the Spirit, the truly repentant person has come to see something of the unattainable righteousness of God and the unsearchable depths of his own depravity. He has been confronted with his sin and made to cry out with the patriarch Job and the apostle Paul:

> If I am condemned,
> Why then do I labor in vain?
> If I wash myself with snow water,
> And cleanse my hands with soap,
> Yet You will plunge me into the pit,
> And my own clothes will abhor me (Job 9:29–31).

Wretched man that I am! Who will deliver me from this body of death? (Rom. 7:24).

This new revelation of self and sin leads even the most self-righteous among people to renounce their trust in their own virtue and merit with

---

32. Ephesians 2:8–9

the same force that they have renounced their most vile and heinous sin. They no longer seek to establish their own righteousness before God by means of works, but "rejoice in Christ Jesus, and have no confidence in the flesh" (Phil. 3:3). This is powerfully illustrated in the conversion of the apostle Paul:

> Though I also might have confidence in the flesh. If anyone else thinks he may have confidence in the flesh, I more so: circumcised the eighth day, of the stock of Israel, of the tribe of Benjamin, a Hebrew of the Hebrews; concerning the law, a Pharisee; concerning zeal, persecuting the church; concerning the righteousness which is in the law, blameless. But what things were gain to me, these I have counted loss for Christ. Yet indeed I also count all things loss for the excellence of the knowledge of Christ Jesus my Lord, for whom I have suffered the loss of all things, and count them as rubbish, that I may gain Christ and be found in Him, not having my own righteousness, which is from the law, but that which is through faith in Christ, the righteousness which is from God by faith (Phil. 3:4–9).

As in the case of grace and works, true repentance and self-righteousness are diametrically opposed and cannot cohabitate in the same person at the same time. The unrepentant person sees himself in "need of nothing." However, when the Spirit of God regenerates his heart and illumines his mind, he sees himself as "wretched, miserable, poor, blind, and naked" (Rev. 3:17). He takes the stance of the publican, who "would not so much as raise his eyes to heaven, but beat his breast, saying, 'God, be merciful to me a sinner!'" (Luke 18:13). He comes to God with the attitude of the old hymn writer who penned:

> Not the labor of my hands,
> Can fulfill Thy law's demands;
> Could my zeal no respite know,
> Could my tears forever flow,
> All for sin could not atone;
> Thou must save, and Thou alone.
> Nothing in my hand I bring,
> Simply to the cross I cling.[33]

The repentant sinner categorically rejects all the deceitful accolades of a works-based religion. Consequently, his heart overflows with the

---

33. Augustus M. Toplady, "Rock of Ages," stanzas 2–3.

words of the psalmist: "Not unto us, O LORD, not unto us, but to Your name give glory" (Ps. 115:1). Any suggestion that he is right with God by virtue of his own character or deeds would horrify him. It would draw from him the following declaration of faith: "God forbid that I should boast except in the cross of our Lord Jesus Christ" (Gal. 6:14).

What place, then, do works have in our salvation? Is the Christian to continue in sin that grace may abound?[34] Is he to be void of fruit and personal righteousness? Absolutely not! Those who have truly repented and believed unto salvation have been regenerated by the Holy Spirit and recreated in the image of Christ. If anyone is in Christ, he is a new creature with a new nature.[35] He has died to sin and been raised to walk in newness of life.[36] By the power of regeneration, the indwelling of the Holy Spirit, and the relentless providence of God, the believer will bear fruit and accomplish good works for the glory of God. However, these good works do not result in salvation; rather, they flow from it. The works the Christian accomplishes, which God prepared beforehand so that he would walk in them, are not the cause of his justification but the evidence of it.

Turning to God in Obedient Submission
Forsaking sin is not an end in itself, but a means to a greater end: a turning to God. Morality is not the same thing as Christianity. Neither does the Christian practice morality for morality's sake, but for God's sake and His glory and delight.[37] Although there is a distinctive Christian or biblical morality, Christianity is primarily about God and an intimate, passionate relationship with Him. Jesus described it in this way: "And this is eternal life, that they may know You, the only true God, and Jesus Christ whom You have sent" (John 17:3).

In using the word *know*, Jesus is not limiting the Christian life to an intellectual endeavor; rather, the knowledge of which He speaks is both relational and intimate. The goal of the Christian life is the pursuit of an intimate knowledge of God that leads to a greater estimation of His worth, a greater satisfaction and joy in His person, and a greater giving of oneself for His glory. As the old catechism states, "Man's chief end is to glorify

---

34. Romans 6:1

35. 2 Corinthians 5:17

36. Romans 6:2–4

37. To practice biblical morality for any reason other than love for God and the promotion of His glory is blatant idolatry.

God and to enjoy Him forever."[38] Therefore, genuine repentance does not stop at turning away from sin, but it is still incomplete until there is a thorough turning to God as the "chief end" of all desire. This truth is especially evident in two Scriptures gleaned from both the Old and New Testaments. The first is from the prophet Isaiah, through whom God declared:

> Seek the LORD while He may be found,
> Call upon Him while He is near.
> Let the wicked forsake his way,
> And the unrighteous man his thoughts;
> Let him return to the LORD,
> And He will have mercy on him;
> And to our God,
> For He will abundantly pardon (Isa. 55:6–7).

It is important to note that this text clearly places the emphasis on returning to the Lord. The renunciation of sin is not an end in itself, but the first step toward the greater end of returning to God. We turn away from sin so that we might turn to Him. The two things are necessary, because God and sin are mutually exclusive. We cannot cherish nor possess both at the same time.

The second text is in Paul's first epistle to the church in Thessalonica. He describes their conversion in the following words: "For they themselves declare concerning us what manner of entry we had to you, and how you turned to God from idols to serve the living and true God, and to wait for His Son from heaven, whom He raised from the dead, even Jesus who delivers us from the wrath to come" (1 Thess. 1:9–10). Once again, it is evident that a person's turning away from sin is secondary to the primary goal of turning to God. The evidence of true conversion among the believers in Thessalonica is that they not only turned from their former idolatry, but they also turned to the living and true God in obedient service. Moreover, they had such a longing for Him that they were patiently awaiting, amid much affliction, His final and full revelation in the second coming of His dear Son. As is the case of all true repentance, there was a "turning away from" and a "turning to." There was a rejection and renunciation of sin and a passionate desire and longing for God.[39]

---

38. Westminster Shorter Catechism, question 1.
39. Other texts that demonstrate the twofold nature of biblical repentance include the following: Isaiah 45:22; Lamentations 3:39–41; Joel 2:12–14; Zechariah 1:3.

Practical Obedience

A life marked by simple and heartfelt obedience to God's commands may be the most obvious and certain proof of true repentance. A person may boast of an inward passion for God and of sincere feelings of piety, but such claims are valid only to the degree that his life conforms to the commandments of Scripture. The strong words of John the Baptist leave no room for misinterpretation. A person is able to make a claim to repentance only to the degree that he bears fruit "worthy of repentance" (Matt. 3:8). A fruitless life proves counterfeit emotional manifestations of contrition. This is a warning to us all, for the axe of God's judgment is already laid at the root of the trees. Every tree that does not bear good fruit is cut down and thrown into the fire. As faith without works is both dead and useless, so repentance without fruit is a powerless counterfeit that cannot save.[40] However, if a person's heart has truly turned Godward, he will evidence it by a newfound practical obedience to the will of God. Even though repentance involves the mind and the emotions, it is ultimately proven true or false by a person's willful submission to God's commands.

Lest we attempt to explain away John the Baptist's warning as an antiquated prophetic message meant for another age, we would do well to remember that his doctrine is also found in the teachings of Jesus and the apostle Paul, respectively:

> Every tree that does not bear good fruit is cut down and thrown into the fire. Therefore by their fruits you will know them. Not everyone who says to Me, "Lord, Lord," shall enter the kingdom of heaven, but he who does the will of My Father in heaven (Matt. 7:19–21).

> Therefore, King Agrippa, I was not disobedient to the heavenly vision, but declared first to those in Damascus and in Jerusalem, and throughout all the region of Judea, and then to the Gentiles, that they should repent, turn to God, and *do works befitting repentance* (Acts 26:19–20, emphasis added).

Scripture strictly condemns any attempt at earning a right standing before God through human merit or works; however, repentance and faith are the result of the supernatural recreating work of the Spirit of God.[41] Such a work of grace will always manifest itself in the transforma-

---

40. Matthew 3:10
41. Galatians 3:10

tion of the believer's life and the bearing of fruit. As the Lord Jesus Christ sets forth in the Sermon on the Mount, those who have truly repented and believed will be known "by their fruits" (Matt. 7:16–20). This does not mean that the truly repentant will always live in perfect conformity to the will of God without the blemish of disobedience. Nor does it insinuate that he will always bear abundant fruit like the blessed man of Psalm 1:3:

> He shall be like a tree
> planted by the rivers of water,
> That brings forth its fruit in its season,
> Whose leaf also shall not wither.

However, it does mean that he will be inclined toward God's commands, and a simple, practical obedience will mark his life. Those who make a claim to repentance without the fruits that most certainly must follow can have little assurance of the validity of their claim and the right standing before God that they suppose.

Continuing and Deepening Work of Repentance

The final characteristic and ultimate test of all genuine repentance is its continuation and growth throughout the believer's life. Through the sanctifying work of the Holy Spirit, the God who begins a work of repentance in us will perfect it; He will see to it that it matures and deepens throughout our lives.[42] This truth is revealed in the very beginning of Christ's teachings recorded in the gospel of Mark: "Jesus came to Galilee, preaching the gospel of the kingdom of God, and saying, 'The time is fulfilled, and the kingdom of God is at hand. Repent, and believe in the gospel'" (1:14–15). In the original Greek text, the commands to repent and believe are both written in the present tense, which indicates continuation. To communicate the proper meaning, Christ's admonition might be translated this way: "The time is fulfilled, and the kingdom of God is at hand; therefore, live a life of repentance and faith in the gospel."

The evidence that a person has truly repented unto salvation is that he continues repenting throughout the full course of his life. Although he must struggle against the flesh, the deceitfulness of sin, and a hardening of the heart, repentance will mark his life. For this reason, in some places of the world, true Christians are scandalously referred to as "repenters"

---

42. Philippians 1:6

because an ever-growing, ever-deepening, ever-maturing repentance marks their lives.[43]

This same truth is set out for us in the Beatitudes, where Christ declares, "Blessed are those who mourn, for they will be comforted" (Matt. 5:4). In this text, the phrase "those who mourn" is translated from a present-tense participle that indicates continuation. Christ is not pronouncing a blessing on those who momentarily or sporadically mourn, but on those whose mourning marks their lives. Although Christ's words need no further validation, they have abundant support throughout the Scriptures. The Lord affirmed the same truth through the prophet Isaiah: "But on this one I will look: on him who is poor and of a contrite spirit, and who trembles at My word" (66:2).

Often in contemporary Christianity, repentance is referred to as something like a flu shot or a vaccination for polio—something that someone does at the moment of conversion and then is done with once and for all. Yet this is contrary to the Scripture's view of repentance. In fact, the evidence that a person has truly repented unto salvation is that he is still repenting today and that his repentance has both increased and deepened since the day of his conversion.

Hardly anyone would object to the truth that we live in a superficial age in which the secular and the religious person seem to walk arm in arm toward the same goal: the pursuit of happiness *in this life*. Consequently, the great taboo in culture and contemporary Christianity is to make mention of anything that might rain on someone's parade, hurt someone's feelings, or undermine someone's self-esteem. People are not only *not* to pursue the Christian graces of repentance, brokenness, and mourning, but they also must avoid them at any cost. For this reason, many among God's children are greatly hindered in their Christian life. They fail to understand that repentance is not only the essential first step toward salvation, but also the very catalyst of true joy.

At conversion, a person begins to see God and himself as never before. This greater revelation of God's holiness and righteousness leads to a greater revelation of self, which, in turn, results in a repentance or brokenness over sin. Nevertheless, the believer is not left in despair, for he is also afforded a greater revelation of the grace of God in the face of

---

43. Evangelical believers in Romania are often referred to as "repenters" by those who are contrary or hostile to their faith.

Christ, which leads to joy unspeakable. This cycle simply repeats itself throughout the Christian life. As the years pass, the Christian sees more of God and more of self, resulting in a greater and deeper brokenness. Yet, all the while, the Christian's joy grows in equal measure because he is privy to greater and greater revelations of the love, grace, and mercy of God in the person and work of Christ. Not only this, but a great interchange occurs in that the Christian learns to rests less and less in his own performance and more and more in the perfect work of Christ. Thus, his joy is not only increased, but it also becomes more consistent and stable. He has left off putting confidence in the flesh, which is idolatry, and is resting in the virtue and merits of Christ, which is true Christian piety.

CHAPTER TWO

A Call to Faith

Jesus came to Galilee, preaching the gospel of the kingdom of God, and saying, "The time is fulfilled, and the kingdom of God is at hand. Repent, and believe in the gospel."

—Mark 1:14–15

But now the righteousness of God apart from the law is revealed, being witnessed by the Law and the Prophets, even the righteousness of God, through faith in Jesus Christ, to all and on all who believe. For there is no difference.

—Romans 3:21–22

Now faith is the substance of things hoped for, the evidence of things not seen.

—Hebrews 11:1

The call to faith, or belief, stands alongside the call of repentance as an essential element in any genuine gospel invitation. Therefore, it is necessary that we have a right understanding of its nature and manifestation in genuine conversion.

BIBLICAL TERMINOLOGY

In the Old Testament, the word *believe* comes from a Hebrew word that means "to stand firm, to trust, to be certain or sure about something."[1] Genesis 15:6 says that Abraham "believed in the LORD, and He accounted it to him for righteousness." That is, Abraham stood firm and trusted in what God had promised him. This same idea is reflected in Habakkuk's famous declaration, "the just shall live by his faith," where the word *faith*

---

1. Hebrew: *aman*.

is translated from the Hebrew word that denotes steadfastness or steadiness (2:4).[2] In the Old Testament, to believe God was to be sure about what He had promised, to trust without wavering, and to stand firm in reliance upon His word.

In the New Testament, the word *believe* is translated from a Greek word that means "to perceive something as true, to be persuaded of it to such a degree that one trusts or places his or her confidence in it."[3] New Testament writers chose this Greek word as the most appropriate to communicate the fullness of the Hebrew idea of faith as confidence in the character and promises of God.

A BIBLICAL DEFINITION

It is a great blessing and demonstration of divine wisdom that the Scriptures do not present faith as an enigma or leave us to our imaginations to discover its meaning. On the contrary, in the Scriptures, God has given us explicit definitions of faith along with many examples and illustrations to clarify its meaning further. The writer of Hebrews penned the most concise of these definitions: "Now faith is the substance of things hoped for, the evidence of things not seen" (11:1).

The word *assurance* comes from a Greek word referring to that which is placed under something, such as substructure or foundation.[4] It came to denote a steadfastness of mind, a firm resolution, a confidence or assurance. The word *conviction* comes from a Greek word that denotes certainty or conviction about the existence or truthfulness of something.[5] In light of the meaning of these terms, we may define biblical faith as the Christian's assurance or confidence that what he hopes for is or will become a reality and the conviction or certainty that what he has not seen actually exists.

This definition of faith, penned under the direction of the Holy Spirit,[6] leaves us with two very important questions: How can we have assurance for what we hope? How can we have the conviction or certainty about something we have never seen? If left unanswered, these

---

2. Hebrew: *emuwnah.*
3. Greek: *pisteúo.*
4. Greek: *hupóstasis.*
5. Greek: *élegchos.*
6. 2 Timothy 3:16; 2 Peter 1:21

two questions could lead the sincere believer into presumption or provide ammunition for the skeptic who rails against faith as nothing more than wishful thinking. After all, a lunatic may have full assurance that he is Lawrence of Arabia, or he may be certain that the lost continent of Atlantis is located just below the subfloor of his house. However, his personal assurance and unwavering conviction do not make it so. How, then, can the Christian have assurance of the salvation for which he hopes, and how can he be certain of the spiritual realities that he has never seen? The answer to these two very important questions is found in the apostle Paul's letter to the church in Rome. Regarding the elderly Abraham's reaction to the promise of a son, he writes that the patriarch was "fully convinced that what [God] had promised He was also able to perform" (Rom. 4:21).

In this text, we find two indispensable elements that make biblical faith something other than presumption or wishful thinking. Abraham was fully assured that he was going to have a son only because he knew God had promised it, and he believed God was both faithful and able to perform it. When Abraham contemplated his own body, he saw that it was as good as dead, being nearly one hundred years old. When he contemplated the body of his wife, Sarah, he knew that conception and childbirth were a natural impossibility.[7] Nevertheless, God had promised Abraham a son, and Abraham "did not waver at the promise of God through unbelief, but was strengthened in faith, giving glory to God" (Rom. 4:20). From this example of Abraham, we learn five important truths about the nature of biblical faith:

1. We can have assurance of what we hope for if God has promised it in His Word.

2. We can have conviction that the things we have not seen are real because God has revealed them or made them known to us in His Word.

3. A lack of assurance about what God has promised or made known in His Word is unbelief.

4. Assurance about something God has not promised is presumption.

---

7. Romans 4:19

5. Genuine biblical faith is not based upon feelings, emotions, or human wisdom but upon what God has revealed or made known to us in His Word.

Before we go on, we must briefly address the skeptic who would argue that our reasoning has one fatal flaw: we are presupposing that our Bible *is* the Word of God. How can we know that this book that we call the Holy Scriptures is God's infallible revelation to humanity, and how can we be sure that its promises apply specifically to us? The answer to these questions is twofold. First, we point to the self-attesting glory of the Bible. Its beauty and wisdom are incomparable. Its extensive scope and perfect unity are unparalleled. Its many prophecies and precise fulfillments are unexplainable apart from divine intervention. Moreover, it offers the only reasonable explanation for the human predicament and the presence of evil. History proves that everything it says about man is true.

Second, we must point to the work of the Holy Spirit, apart from which faith is impossible. The great majority of Christians come to faith in Christ without the aid of apologetics. Furthermore, most who have died as martyrs for their faith could not have given a reason for the hope that was within them by employing the classical arguments of apologetics. What, then, was the basis of their faith in the Bible and its gospel? The answer is the regenerating and illuminating work of the Holy Spirit. The Christian believes that the Bible is the Word of God because the Holy Spirit has revealed it to him. As in the case of Lydia from the city of Thyatira, the Lord has opened the Christian's heart to respond in faith to the Word.[8]

This is why the rural tribesman in the most remote part of the world will die a martyr before he will deny the Scriptures. He knows they are true and worth dying for because God has made it known to him. This uneducated, defenseless tribesman has assurance of the salvation he hopes for and the certain conviction of the spiritual realities he has never seen, because through the regenerating and illuminating work of the Holy Spirit, God has taught him.[9]

---

8. "Now a certain woman named Lydia heard us. She was a seller of purple from the city of Thyatira, who worshiped God. The Lord opened her heart to heed the things spoken by Paul" (Acts 16:14).

9. Isaiah 54:13; Jeremiah 31:34; John 6:45

Both the beauty and scandal of biblical Christianity are found in this truth. Although apologetics is extremely helpful in evangelism and the strengthening of the believer's faith, our faith is not dependent upon our ability to answer all the questions or to refute skeptics. We believe in the Bible and the gospel because the God who said, "Let light shine out of darkness" is the same God who has shone in our hearts to give the light of the knowledge of the glory of God in the face of Christ.[10] This truth provides a sure direction for the preacher, who may employ the greatest arguments to defend the gospel but understands the gospel itself is the power of God unto salvation.[11]

FAITH IN CHRIST

To become recipients of God's great work of salvation, we must not only repent of our sins, but we must also believe or trust in what God has done for us though His Son, Jesus Christ. We must forsake all other confidences and place our trust exclusively in the person and work of Jesus Christ, His death on the cross for our sins, and His resurrection from the dead. We must believe that what He did, He did for us and that we have been reconciled to God and given eternal life in Him.

It is important to understand that as God commands all men everywhere to repent of their sins, He likewise commands all men everywhere to believe in His Son.[12] In his first epistle, the apostle John wrote: "And this is His commandment: that we should believe on the name of His Son Jesus Christ" (3:23). When the multitudes asked Jesus what they must do to "work the works of God," He responded, "This is the work of God, that you believe in Him whom He sent" (John 6:28–29). It is also important to understand that people can obey the command to believe in Jesus Christ only to the exclusion of all other objects of faith. To believe that Jesus is the Savior of the world is to disbelieve all others who make a similar claim. This is possibly the most scandalous demand of the Christian faith. A person cannot make a claim of saving faith in Christ as Savior without the absolute rejection of any other means. Genuine faith does not trust in Jesus Christ as *a* Savior, but as *the* Savior.

---

10. 2 Corinthians 4:6
11. Romans 1:16
12. Acts 17:30

This claim is not the narrow-minded invention of a radical funda-
mentalism, but rather finds it origins in the teachings of Christ and His
apostles. Jesus pointed to Himself and declared, "I am the way, the truth,
and the life. No one comes to the Father except through Me" (John 14:6).
The apostle Peter was just as bold when he stood on trial before the San-
hedrin and announced, "Nor is there salvation in any other, for there is
no other name under heaven given among men by which we must be
saved" (Acts 4:12). The apostle Paul admonished the young Timothy to do
the work of an evangelist and to suffer hardship as a good soldier of Jesus
Christ,[13] knowing that there is "one God and one Mediator between God
and men, the Man Christ Jesus" (1 Tim. 2:5). Based upon these verses, it is
not unfair or hypercritical to say that any supposed minister of the gospel who does not deny the possibility of salvation through all but Jesus
Christ has denied the faith. He has brought Christ's terrible warning of
judgment upon his own head: "But whoever denies Me before men, him I
will also deny before My Father who is in heaven" (Matt. 10:33).

God has provided only one scarlet thread by which we may safely
swing out into eternity: Christ and His bloody death on the cross of Calvary. To repeat the words of the apostle Peter, "Nor is there salvation in
any other" (Acts 4:12). Only this gospel bears God's approval.

FAITH TO THE GLORY OF GOD

In Romans, the apostle Paul makes an insightful remark regarding a
result or outcome of genuine faith. He writes: "[Abraham] did not waver
at the promise of God through unbelief, but was strengthened in faith,
giving glory to God" (4:20, emphasis added). It is apparent that Abraham's
faith not only glorified God through the worship that accompanied it
but also that his faith itself brought glory to God. The key to understanding this truth is in the book of Hebrews. The writer tells us: "But
without faith it is impossible to please Him, for he who comes to God
must believe that He is, and that He is a rewarder of those who diligently
seek Him" (11:6).

Our faith pleases God and brings glory to Him because it is a personal
declaration regarding the integrity of His character. When we respond in
faith to the Word of God, we are manifesting that we have the greatest

---

13. 2 Timothy 2:3; 4:5

confidence in everything that God says about Himself. To believe Him is to give personal testimony to humans and angels that He is a God of faithfulness and without injustice; that His work is perfect and all His ways are just; that He keeps His covenant and His lovingkindness to a thousand generations; and that it is impossible for Him to lie.[14] On the other hand, unbelief is a direct affront upon the character of God. It casts doubt upon His works in the past, and it questions His integrity in the present: Does He really exist? Is He really the rewarder of those who seek Him? Did He really make such a promise? Such questions put God on trial by submitting His claims to human scrutiny. They are spawned from the heart of the devil and are the very means used to murder our first parents.[15] To disbelieve God is to bring the whole of who He is into question, but to believe Him is to affirm His testimony regarding Himself and to bring Him glory.

Regarding the gospel, this truth has great implications. God has set His seal upon all His works in history and has confirmed them by many great and undisputable evidences. However, God has given His greatest testimony with regard to His Son. Therefore, the one who believes in the Son believes in God and does His will, but the one who does not believe in the Son has made God a liar and is hostile to Him. The apostle John writes:

> If we receive the witness of men, the witness of God is greater; for this is the witness of God which He has testified of His Son. He who believes in the Son of God has the witness in himself; he who does not believe God has made Him a liar, because he has not believed the testimony that God has given of His Son. And this is the testimony: that God has given us eternal life, and this life is in His Son. He who has the Son has life; he who does not have the Son of God does not have life (1 John 5:9–12).

Guided by the Holy Spirit, John offers impeccable logic. First, he argues for the credibility of God's testimony over that of any man. The Scriptures declare that all men are liars,[16] but God "is not a man that He should lie, nor a son of man, that He should repent" (Num. 23:19). There-fore, if we daily believe the testimony of men, how much more should we believe the testimony of God? Second, John affirms that God has

---

14. Numbers 23:19; Deuteronomy 7:9; 32:4; Titus 1:2; Hebrews 6:18
15. Genesis 3:1–6; John 8:44
16. Romans 3:4

indeed given testimony concerning His Son, and His testimony is this: that everything pertaining to salvation, fellowship with God, and eternal life is found in Jesus Christ alone. Finally, John comes to His radical and unbending conclusion that anyone who does not fully embrace the Son has no hope of eternal life, and anyone who does not believe in the Son has made God a liar. Apart from Jesus Christ, people have no part with God. This is the testimony of apostolic Christianity: "Whoever denies the Son does not have the Father either; he who acknowledges the Son has the Father also" (1 John 2:23).

We most please and glorify God, then, by believing, trusting, and relying upon the very thing to which He has given His greatest testimony: that Jesus of Nazareth is His beloved Son in whom He is well pleased; that He is the way, the truth, and the life, and no one comes to the Father but through Him.[17] The one who believes and confesses such things about the Son both pleases God and brings glory to His name. The one who refuses to believe has declared God to be a liar and has forfeited any possibility of eternal life.

THE END OF BOASTING

The very instant that even the most minute work is added to or mingled with the doctrine of salvation, Christianity becomes a works religion, justification becomes a thing to be earned, God becomes the debtor of people, and people are able to boast before Him. This is why the apostle Paul labors with all his might in his writings to accentuate the depravity of humanity and prove their utter inability to please God in the flesh. He desires that "every mouth may be stopped, and all the world may become guilty before God" (Rom. 3:19). Only then will people turn their eyes from themselves and look to God in faith. Only then will they cease from works and fall into the arms of grace. Only then will their boasting in self become a boasting in God. "As it is written, 'He who glories, let him glory in the LORD'" (1 Cor. 1:31).

In Romans 3, Paul sets forth these truths with inspired clarity. In the first two-thirds of the chapter, he labors to prove that all people are sinners and stand condemned before a righteous God and His law.[18] Then

17. Matthew 3:17; 17:5; Mark 9:7; John 14:6; 2 Peter 1:17
18. Romans 3:1–20

he shifts his attention to the work of Christ on Calvary and sets before us the most majestic truths recorded in the Scriptures. He portrays Christ as the great propitiation who bore the sins of His people, suffered the wrath of God in their place, and made it possible for a just God to justify wicked people without betraying His own righteousness.[19] Finally, Paul concludes with the following exclamation: "Where is boasting then? It is excluded. By what law? Of works? No, but by the law of faith. Therefore we conclude that a man is justified by faith apart from the deeds of the law" (Rom. 3:27–28).

Paul closes his argument with this rhetorical question: "Where is boasting then?" Before anyone can raise a hand or give an answer, he answers his own question with an exclamation that demonstrates unbending conviction and the firmest resolution: "It is excluded." The phrase may also be translated, "It has been shut out or turned outdoors."[20] Here, Paul uses the aorist tense to communicate that boasting in works as a means of salvation has been absolutely or in a decisive manner shut out to preclude any further debate on the matter.[21] It is as though Paul is saying, "Of works? Do not even think it, let alone argue the matter. It has been excluded once and for all as a means of right standing before God."

It is important to note that not all boasting is excluded, but only that which has to do with human merit. Although there is no room for boasting in our works, or even in our faith, there are both grounds and room for boasting in God and His grace. When we are asked for "a reason for the hope that is in [us]" (1 Peter 3:15), we must emphatically declare, "It is all of grace!"[22]

> Having predestined us to adoption as sons by Jesus Christ to Himself, according to the good pleasure of His will, to the praise of the glory of His grace, by which He made us accepted in the Beloved (Eph. 1:5–6).

> For by grace you have been saved through faith, and that not of yourselves; it is the gift of God, not of works, lest anyone should boast (Eph. 2:8–9).

---

19. Romans 3:21–26

20. Joseph Henry Thayer, *Thayers Greek-English Lexicon* (Grand Rapids: Baker, 1977), 195.

21. Paul uses the aorist tense form of *ekkleío*, denoting that "[boasting] is peremptorily, or once for all, shut out." W. Robertson Nicoll, *The Expositor's Greek Testament* (London: Hodder and Stoughton, 1897–1910), 2:613.

22. Thought taken from *All of Grace: An Earnest Word with Those Who Are Seeking Salvation by the Lord Jesus Christ,* by Charles Spurgeon (Pasadena, Tex.: Pilgrim Publications, 1978).

> Not unto us, O LORD, not unto us,
> But to Your name give glory,
> Because of Your mercy,
> Because of Your truth (Ps. 115:1).

By nature, humans are full of vanity, self-conceit, and boasting. The spirit of Lamech and Haman lives in us all.[23] We boast of our wisdom, strength, and status, yet we do not notice that we are but one nose-full of air, our existence is like a vapor, our wisdom is folly, and our righteousness is like filthy rags.[24] For this reason, the prophet Jeremiah warns us:

> Thus says the LORD:
> "Let not the wise man glory in his wisdom,
> Let not the mighty man glory in his might,
> Nor let the rich man glory in his riches;
> But let him who glories glory in this,
> That he understands and knows Me,
> That I am the LORD, exercising lovingkindness,
>   judgment, and righteousness in the earth.
> For in these I delight," says the LORD (Jer. 9:23–24).

According to the Scriptures, people never have grounds for boasting. Whatever noble thing they might attain can be attributed only to the grace of God. Whatever fault or weakness found in them is their own doing. That which is worth boasting about is not theirs, and that which is theirs is not worth boasting about. This is especially true with regard to salvation and a right standing before God. Any person who has seen anything of the righteousness of God and of his own sin must "conclude that a man is justified by faith apart from the deeds of the law" (Rom. 3:28). The word *maintain* comes from a Greek word that means "to reckon, compute, calculate, reason, or conclude."[25] A true reckoning of the contents of our hearts and a proper calculation of our merits and vices should lead any of us to conclude that if salvation is through the works of the law, then we are utterly without hope. The smallest revelation of our sinfulness in the light of God's righteousness should cause any of us to join the desperate choir of others who have had similar painful glimpses of themselves in light of God's glory:

---

23. Genesis 4:23–24; Esther 5:11
24. Isaiah 2:22; 64:6; James 4:14
25. Greek: *logízomai.*

Job: "I have heard of You by the hearing of the ear,
But now my eye sees You.
Therefore I abhor myself,
And repent in dust and ashes" (42:5–6).

Isaiah: "Woe is me, for I am undone!
Because I am a man of unclean lips,
And I dwell in the midst of a people of unclean lips;
For my eyes have seen the King,
The LORD of hosts" (6:5).

Paul: "O wretched man that I am! Who will deliver
me from this body of death?" (Rom. 7:24).

The sinner must come to an essential crisis point in which he sees that he is utterly destitute of saving merit and that, search as he may, he finds no hope of salvation in himself. Only then will he turn to grace and call upon mercy. In other words, we must all join the publicans and sinners if we expect to be saved.[26] "For as many as are of the works of the law are under the curse" (Gal. 3:10), but blessed is the one to whom God credits righteousness by faith apart from works:

Blessed are those whose lawless deeds are forgiven,
And whose sins are covered;
Blessed is the man to whom the LORD shall not impute
sin (Rom. 4:6–8).

A true knowledge of God and self is essential in the conversion of the sinner, but it is also equally essential in the ongoing sanctification of the saint. The believer must continue to grow in his knowledge of God and self until he becomes so convinced of grace alone that he would be disgusted at the mere suggestion that his salvation might be the result of his own virtue, merit, or piety. In fact, this is one of the greatest purposes and results of God's work of sanctification in the life of the believer. Throughout the full course of our lives, He is orchestrating all things to destroy our self-righteousness and self-confidence so that we might rely upon the virtue of Christ's person and the merit of His perfect work on Calvary. He does this for His glory and our good. Our spiritual welfare and fruitfulness depend on this interchange of self-confidence for reliance upon God alone. The prophet Jeremiah puts it this way:

---

26. Luke 18:13–14

> Cursed is the man who trusts in man
> And makes flesh his strength,
> Whose heart departs from the LORD.
> For he shall be like a shrub in the desert,
> And shall not see when good comes,
> But shall inhabit the parched places in the wilderness,
> In a salt land which is not inhabited.
> Blessed is the man who trusts in the LORD,
> And whose hope is the LORD.
> For he shall be like a tree planted by the waters,
> Which spreads out its roots by the river,
> And will not fear when heat comes;
> But its leaf will be green,
> And will not be anxious in the year of drought,
> Nor will cease from yielding fruit (Jer. 17:5–8).

In conclusion, I am astounded to see how people in the same congregation react to a message that emphasizes human depravity, the lack of saving merit in their works, and their desperate need of divine grace. Some are downcast, others are offended, and still others are outright angry that such harsh words would be spoken about them and their pious efforts. Yet others in the same congregation who hear the same truths are full of joy and rejoice in the goodness of God. The darker the preacher paints them, the more joyous they become and the greater their praise. What is the difference between the two groups? Those among the first group have placed their confidence in the flesh and boast in their own virtue and merit. Those of the second group are "the circumcision, who worship God in the Spirit, rejoice in Christ Jesus, and have no confidence in the flesh" (Phil. 3:3). They are content to have their darkness exposed if through such an ordeal Christ and the grace of God might be exalted. They know that the darkness of their night brings the stars of God's grace into greater view.

CHAPTER THREE

Believe and Confess

But the righteousness of faith speaks in this way, "Do not say in your heart, 'Who will ascend into heaven?' (that is, to bring Christ down from above) or, 'Who will descend into the abyss?' (that is, to bring Christ up from the dead). But what does it say? "The word is near you, in your mouth and in your heart" (that is, the word of faith which we preach): that if you confess with your mouth the Lord Jesus and believe in your heart that God has raised Him from the dead, you will be saved. For with the heart one believes unto righteousness, and with the mouth confession is made unto salvation.

—Romans 10:6–10

This is arguably one of the most eloquent and important passages in the Scriptures regarding what a person must do to be saved.[1] Throughout the centuries of Christianity, it has served as a source of comfort for all who believe and as a wall of defense against the almost constant barrage of every false teaching that would seek to mingle works with faith as the means of salvation. A person does not win salvation by any valiant deed or noble pilgrimage, but by calling upon the name of the Lord in faith.

A NEAR WORD

In the first five verses of Romans 10, the apostle Paul demonstrates the great theological error of many in the nation of Israel. Though they had a commendable zeal, they did not seek a right standing before God by faith in the atoning work of His Son. Instead, they sought righteousness through a rigorous and excruciating obedience to the law.[2] Paul counters their false view by declaring that the perfect saving work of Christ

---

1. Acts 16:30
2. Romans 10:1–3

marked the end of all attempts to establish a person's own righteousness before God through human merit or effort.[3]

The law places demands upon fallen people that they cannot accomplish any more than they can "ascend into heaven" or "descend into the abyss." However, faith is entirely different. It requires no heroic feat or impossible religious conformity. Instead, it calls a person to acknowledge his "helpless estate" and to rest upon the person and accomplishments of Christ.[4] This is why the apostle Paul assures the Christians in Rome that everything they required for a right standing before God was appropriated to them through their faith in the "word" of the gospel that had been brought "near" to them through the apostolic preaching.[5] They could rest assured of their salvation because they had believed in their hearts the gospel message that was preached to them, and they were openly confessing Jesus as Lord.

THE MISUSE OF THE TEXT

This passage has rightly become one of the most popular and most employed among modern-day evangelists and those who seek to share their faith with others. However, what does it truly mean, and what is its proper application in evangelism? Can a person fulfill these biblical requirements of believing and confessing merely by making a decision for Christ, praying the sinner's prayer, or confessing Christ before a congregation of affirming believers? To answer these questions, we must consider Paul's words in their proper context and determine the precise meaning of his language. We must be wary of assuming that a text means a certain thing or should be used a certain way simply because our contemporaries hold to a prevalent interpretation and application of the text. We often assume that we understand a text because we received an interpretation of it without question from those who received it without question from others. However, when someone actually studies the text "to find out whether these things [are] so," this naïve chain of unquestioned trust is often broken (Acts 17:11). We would do well, then, to ask ourselves this question: Did the apostle Paul write this text with the

---

3. Romans 10:4
4. From "It Is Well With My Soul,"stanza 2, by Horatio Gates Spafford (1828–1888).
5. I.e., "had been made readily available to them."

purpose of giving us a model for the sinner's prayer, or did he have an entirely different purpose in mind?

In contemporary evangelicalism, the sinner's prayer has become the foremost means of inviting people to Christ and granting them assurance of salvation. It is found on the back of most evangelistic tracts and heard at the end of many evangelistic sermons. It usually includes the following elements: the seeker is led to confess that he is a sinner and to acknowledge his inability to save himself. He is then directed to confess that Jesus died for his sins and rose again from the dead. Subsequently, he is encouraged to ask Jesus to come into his heart and to be his Savior. Afterward, he is promised that if he prayed this prayer sincerely, he is now saved. Finally, he is assured that if he ever doubts his salvation, he should stand upon this moment when he prayed the sinner's prayer and confessed Christ.

Although there is some truth in these various elements, there are several serious objections that we should raise to this method of inviting sinners to Christ. First, it has no biblical precedent. It was not employed by Christ, the apostles, or the early Christians. Second, it was unknown to most of the church throughout history. It is a recent invention. Third, it has the danger of turning the gospel into a creedal statement. Numerous individuals who show no biblical evidence of conversion believe themselves saved simply because at one time in their lives they made a decision for Christ and repeated the sinner's prayer. Although Christians who use the sinner's prayer in evangelism do not intend this, it has been the overwhelming result of this methodology. Fourth, it has almost entirely replaced the biblical invitation of repentance and faith. It is astounding that the biblical examples of inviting people to Christ are virtually ignored in favor of a modern-day construct. Fifth, it has become the primary and, often, only basis of assurance. That is, many individuals who bear little or no evidence of God's work in their lives are convinced or assured of their salvation only because once they prayed the sinner's prayer sincerely.

This popular application of Romans 10:9 to the seeker is contrary to Paul's logic and purpose. It distorts one of the most powerful teachings of the Scriptures on *sola fide*[6] and one of its most powerful promises to the

---

6. Latin: "faith alone." This historic phrase refers to salvation by faith alone in the redemptive work of God through Jesus Christ without any mixture of human merit. It is

people of God. It has also turned the text into an empty creed that people have used to give a false assurance of salvation to countless individuals who bear little fruit of conversion. For these reasons, it is imperative that we take a thorough look at this text in light of its grammatical and historical context.

To grasp something of Paul's meaning and purpose, it is helpful to understand that he is referring to both a one-time event in the believer's life and to the result or fruit of that event, which continues throughout the entirety of the believer's life. In other words, he is speaking of a person's conversion experience and of the ongoing fruit of that conversion, which validates it or demonstrates it to be genuine. A sinner is justified and reconciled with God the moment he truly believes in the person and atoning work of Christ. However, the evidence that he truly believed and was genuinely converted in that moment is that he goes on believing and confessing all the days of his life. This is not to say that the true believer will be immune to doubts, free from failure, or unhindered in his growth to maturity. However, it does mean that the God who began a good work in him will continue perfecting that work until the final day.[7] Salvation is by grace alone through faith alone.[8] However, the evidence of saving faith is a genuine and enduring confession of the lordship of Jesus Christ throughout the believer's life.

Herein lies the problem with the modern-day use of this text. No one can deny that there are many individuals in the street and pew who believe they are saved because one time in their lives they supposedly believed in their heart and confessed with their mouth, but there is little abiding fruit. They live the full course of their lives in carnality and worldliness without any real evidence of the enduring power of God, which Scripture teaches will always accompany salvation. Yet they are adamant in their convictions because one time in their lives, they "made their decision" and "prayed the prayer." Evangelical ministers who validate such individuals' salvation further exacerbate the problem. They base their confirmation upon a supposed conversion experience but neglect to consider whether there is any evidence of an ongoing work

---

one of the five *solas* that summarize the theological beliefs of the Reformation. The other four *solas* are *sola Scriptura* (by Scripture alone), *sola gratia* (by grace alone), *solus Christus* (Christ alone), *soli Deo gloria* (glory to God alone).

7. Philippians 1:6

8. Ephesians 2:8

of sanctification or the bearing of fruit. It seems they have forgotten a foundational truth of the gospel: genuine saving faith is validated by its perseverance and fruit, and the evidence that we have been saved from the condemnation of sin is that we are currently being saved from the power of sin.[9]

BELIEVING WITH THE HEART

In Romans 10:9–10, the apostle Paul says you are saved if you believe "in your heart" and "with the heart." If our salvation depends on such faith, then our consideration and correct interpretation of these two phrases are of utmost importance. Before we begin any discussion regarding faith, we would do well to remember that the demons also believe and tremble, but not unto salvation.[10] When Jesus began preaching in Galilee, the demons who had possessed a certain man in the synagogue cried out, "I know who You are—the Holy One of God!" (Mark 1:24). The Gerasene demoniac spoke in even greater detail when he confessed that Jesus was the "Son of the Most High God" (Mark 5:7). Scripture, then, suggests that Satan and the demons have an acute knowledge of the person and work of Jesus Christ and accept them as absolute realities. They know He is the Son of God, that He died on Calvary for the sins of His people, and that He rose again on the third day. However, their knowledge and recognition of the realities of Christ do not lead to their salvation. They are not saved by what they know to be true, but rather they are condemned by it. This same malady is found among humans.

Any honest evaluation of contemporary evangelicalism will acknowledge that there are many people walking the streets and sitting in pews who have "obtained like precious faith with us" as the demons (2 Peter 1:1).[11] They know something of the person and work of Christ, and they will make something of a confession when it is convenient. However, there is little evidence of an ongoing reality of the saving work of Christ in their lives. Their hope of eternal salvation is founded upon a decision they made long ago, which they believed was sincere, to "accept Christ" by means of a simple prayer. Ministers of the gospel who should

---

9. Mark 13:13; Philippians 1:6; James 2:18

10. James 2:19

11. In this passage, genuine Christians are referred to as "those who have obtained like precious faith with us [the apostles]."

have known better confirmed their hope. Like demons, they are lost. Yet, unlike demons, they do not know it.

Now that we have seen the dangers of a heartless faith, we are ready to examine a true faith of the heart—one that not only recognizes what is true about the person and work of Christ but also relies upon these realities and is transformed by them. In the Scriptures, the heart refers to the very core, or essence, of a person. It is the seat of one's intellect, will, and emotions. In one sense, we can say the heart is the control center of all we are. What happens there affects everything else about us. Therefore, it is absurd to think that a person could believe something "in" or "with" the heart without it also having a dramatic or even drastic effect upon the totality of his person.

To believe in our heart that God raised Jesus from the dead is to believe with our innermost being that everything Jesus said about Himself is true. This may not sound too radical until we consider some of the things that He actually said:

- He is the eternal God and the creator of the universe.[12]
- He is the life and light of all men.[13]
- He is humankind's only savior.[14]
- He is the absolute sovereign of the universe.[15]
- He will determine the eternal destiny of all men.[16]
- He is more valuable than the combined wealth of the world.[17]
- The promotion of His will and agenda is the purpose of the universe and of every individual's life.[18]
- He is to be loved above all other persons and things.[19]
- He is to be radically followed and obeyed no matter the cost.[20]
- He will judge His people's service to Him and reward them accordingly.[21]

---

12. John 1:1–2; 8:58–59
13. John 1:4; 6:35; 8:12; 11:25
14. John 8:24; 14:6; Acts 4:12
15. Matthew 28:18; Acts 2:36
16. Matthew 16:27; 25:31–46
17. Matthew 16:26
18. Luke 6:46; 12:47
19. Luke 14:26
20. Matthew 16:24–25; Luke 14:27–33
21. Matthew 16:27; 2 Corinthians 5:10

These radical claims of Christ do not leave room for a nonchalant response, nor can we believe them at the center of our intellect, will, and emotions without experiencing a radical, or even devastating effect upon our lives. It is impossible for a rational creature to embrace these truths and not be noticeably changed by them. The very nature of the claims demands a cataclysmic change in the character of one's person and the direction of his life.

Therefore, true saving faith is not a passive or partial reliance upon Christ, but a reliance that is active and growing. Through the continuing work of sanctification, it eventually encompasses the entirety of the believer's life. The proof of saving faith is not that once upon a time we merely "accepted Christ" through a prayer we repeated by rote, but that since the moment we first believed the gospel, Christ's claims about Himself and His claim upon us continue to be a greater reality in our lives.

CONFESSING WITH THE MOUTH

Having taken a brief glance at heartfelt faith, we must now consider what it means to confess with the mouth. The first thing we should notice from Romans 10:9–10 is the specificity of the confession. It is not merely a confession of faith in Jesus Christ but a confession of His absolute and universal lordship. Thus, the evidence that a person has believed with his heart and is trusting in the saving virtue of the person and work of Christ is that he is also confessing Him as Lord.

The long history of Christianity proves that nothing could be more radical or costly than to confess *Kúrios Iesous,* which is Greek for "Jesus is Lord!" In the Roman world, there was only one lord, and his name was Caesar. Even to mention the possibility of another was political treason, often resulting in exile or execution. In the Jewish religion, there was only one Lord, and His name was Yahweh. To give the title of "lord" to another was blasphemous and worthy of death. The renowned Greek scholar A. T. Robertson writes, "No Jew would do this who had not really trusted Christ, for *kúrios* [lord] in the LXX[22] is used of God. No Gentile would do it who had not ceased worshipping the emperor as *kúrios*."[23] Robertson

---

22. The abbreviated symbol for the Septuagint—the Greek translation of the Old Testament Scriptures.

23. A. T. Robertson, *Word Pictures in the New Testament* (Nashville: Broadman Press, 1930–1933), 4:389.

continues, "One is reminded of the demand made to Polycarp that he say *Kúrios Kaisar* [Caesar is lord] and how each time he replied *Kúrios Iesous.* He paid the penalty for his loyalty with his life. Lighthearted men today can say 'Lord Jesus' in a flippant or even in an irreverent way, but no Jew or Gentile then said it who did not mean it."[24]

We are saved by faith alone in the person and work of Christ, but the evidence that our faith is genuine is our confession of the lordship of Jesus Christ and our allegiance to Him, even when such a confession costs us dearly. The early church suffered and died because it faithfully proclaimed Jesus as Lord and refused to worship Caesar. At this moment, Christians suffer imprisonment, torture, and death because of the same confession. Even in the Western world, where there is little or no physical persecution to speak of, the true believer is the one who submits to the lordship of Jesus Christ rather than live by the standards of "this present evil age" (Gal. 1:4). This is the apostle Paul's meaning when he writes, "If you confess with your mouth the Lord Jesus and believe in your heart that God has raised Him from the dead, you will be saved" (Rom. 10:9).

True faith in Jesus shows itself in a real submission to and an open confession of His lordship, which deepens as the believer matures and grows stronger even in the most adverse of circumstances. The great evidence of salvation is that a person continues on to maturity in this same faith and confession. Commenting on Romans 10:9–10, the renowned Scottish Baptist Robert Haldane (1764–1842) writes:

> A man becomes righteous, perfectly righteous, through believing God's record concerning His Son. But the evidence that this faith is genuine is found in the open confession of the Lord with the mouth in everything in which His will is known. Confession of Christ is as necessary as faith in Him, but necessary for a different purpose. Faith is necessary to obtain the gift of righteousness. Confession is necessary to prove that this gift is received. If a man does not confess Christ at that hazard of life, character, property, liberty, and everything dear to him, he has not the faith of Christ. In saying, then, that confession is made unto salvation, the apostle does not mean that it is the cause of salvation, or that without it the title to salvation is incomplete. When a man believes in his heart, he is justified. But confession of Christ is the effect of faith, and will be evidence of it at

---

24. Robertson, *Word Pictures*, 4:168.

the last day. Faith which interests the sinner in the righteousness of Christ is manifested by the confession of His name in the midst of enemies, or in the face of danger.[25]

CONFESSION IN ITS HISTORICAL CONTEXT

In order for us to understand what Paul meant when he wrote of the necessity of confessing Jesus as Lord, it is helpful to consider what it meant to the Christians of the early church. A letter from Pliny the Younger, governor of Bithynia, to the Roman emperor Trajan (r. 98–117), briefly describes how those accused of being Christian were interrogated and charges against them either proven or dismissed: "An anonymous information was laid before me, containing a charge against several persons, who upon examination denied they were Christians or had ever been so. They repeated after me an invocation to the gods, and offered religious rites with wine and incense before your statue, and even reviled the name of Christ.... I thought it proper, therefore, to discharge them."[26]

Pliny writes of several people who were obviously falsely accused of being followers of Christ. In proof of their innocence, they called upon the Roman gods, offered worship to the emperor, and reviled the name of Jesus. They did the very opposite of what Romans 10:9–10 says a Christian would do.

Although the content of Pliny's letter provides us with an example of those who were innocent of being Christian, it does give us a solid foundation for supposing how the scenario would have turned out differently if the accused had truly been Christian. Imagine that Roman authorities discovered a small house church and brought them before the Roman official. In order to prove or disprove the accusation against them, they are led to a small altar, where they are commanded to perform a few simple rituals. First, they must call upon the Roman gods. Second, they must participate in a form of emperor worship to prove their loyalty to Caesar. Finally, they are told to revile Christ, either to deny His lordship or to declare Him accursed.[27] To the horror of the small fellowship, two of their own promptly take their place before the altar and do as they

---

25. Robert Haldane, *Exposition of the Epistle to the Romans* (Edinburgh: Banner of Truth, 1958), 508.

26. Merrill C. Tenney, *New Testament Times* (Grand Rapids: Eerdmans, 1965), 329–30.

27. 1 Corinthians 12:3

are commanded. As they are discharged, another is forced to his feet and commanded to obey. Though full of fear and trembling, he not only refuses to venerate the Roman gods and Caesar, but he replies "*Kúrios Iesous*," "Jesus is Lord!" He is taken away by force to await either exile or execution. One by one, the rest of the fellowship makes the same faithful confession, and their fate is sealed. Though this is a fictional scenario, the archives of Christian history prove that countless believers have faced such testing and prevailed at the cost of their own lives. Their testing proved that they believed in their heart unto salvation because they confessed Jesus as Lord even unto death.

A PROPER APPLICATION

In light of the true significance of Romans 10:9–10 and what truly confessing Christ has cost so many followers of Jesus through the ages, its popular use in modern-day evangelism is indefensible. To suggest that this text is the biblical foundation for the sinner's prayer that concludes many evangelistic tracts and sermons is a serious exegetical fallacy. Yet because of this popular belief, many unconverted men, women, and children have an almost impenetrable assurance of their eternal salvation simply because at one time in their lives they affirmed a few biblical truths and repeated a model prayer. Afterward, there was no transformation, no continuing work of sanctification, no rejection of the world, and no desire for Christ. Borrowing from the apostle Paul, it is proper to ask, "You foolish evangelicals, who has bewitched you?"[28]

Romans 10:6–10 teaches us that we are saved by faith alone. Christians do not earn salvation by some heroic feat or exhausting endeavor; rather, they receive it by faith in the person and work of Christ. Those who truly believe have long given up any and every attempt to establish their own righteousness. They have fallen upon Christ, and upon His virtue and merit they stand.

However, this faith in Christ is not temporary, static, or undetectable, but persevering, dynamic, and evident. This is ensured because salvation is the work of God for the glory of God. He who first wrought saving faith in the heart of the believer will see to it that that faith perseveres, deepens, and manifests. One such manifestation will be the confession

---

28. Galatians 3:1

of the lordship of Jesus Christ through both word and deed—regardless of the cost!

How, then, should we employ and apply these verses? For the believer, it should be a constant consolation and warning. The consolation is that we are saved by grace alone through faith alone. Our right standing before God is not the result of our strenuous efforts or mighty deeds, but rather the result of Christ's great effort and mighty accomplishment on Calvary. The warning is that one of the chief evidences of saving faith and true conversion is the growing reality of Christ's lordship in our lives and our willingness to follow Him, even at the greatest cost. With regard to evangelism and our treatment of the seeker, these verses should be used in a threefold manner. First, we should use them to prove to the seeker the uselessness of works and admonish him to lay aside all hope of gaining salvation through personal virtue or merit. Second, we should employ them to encourage him to look to Christ alone and to believe in Him unto salvation. Third, the seeker should use them as an ongoing litmus test for the genuineness of his profession. He should know that if he is truly converted, the lordship of Jesus Christ will become a growing reality in his life. Although he will pass through great struggles and suffer many failures in his faith, piety, and confession throughout his life, his identity and purpose will be increasingly bound up in the mastery of Christ over him.

CHAPTER FOUR

Receiving Christ

But as many as received Him, to them He gave the right to become children of God, to those who believe in His name.

—John 1:12

Behold, I stand at the door and knock. If anyone hears My voice and opens the door, I will come in to him and dine with him, and he with Me.

—Revelation 3:20

Modern-day evangelism emphasizes a person's making a decision, praying the sinner's prayer, and receiving Jesus Christ into his heart. These steps have become so ingrained in the modern evangelical mind that it seems almost impossible to do evangelism without them. However, in spite of their widespread acceptance, we must ask ourselves if such a methodology is truly scriptural. Since John 1:12 and Revelation 3:20 are most often cited as the biblical foundation for this form of contemporary evangelism, it will be helpful to examine each text carefully in this chapter and the next. Do they support a method of evangelism that assures people of eternal salvation simply because they have made a one-time decision for Christ, opened up their hearts by a free act of their will, and received Jesus through prayer?

Before we consider these texts, we must once again fully recognize the seriousness of our endeavor. Many would agree that the most common maladies among evangelicals in the West are empty professions and rampant carnality. There are millions of people convinced of their salvation because they have followed the "steps," yet they continue in worldliness, without the slightest desire for the things of God. What is the reason for this? Is salvation so weak that it has no effect upon a person unless he follows up with a lifetime of intensive personal discipleship and accountability? Or, is there another, sadder reason: many of our supposed converts are not converted at all? Could it be that our lack of knowledge of the gospel is leading to the destruction of millions? Have we unknowingly become like the false prophets of old who healed the people superficially, saying, "'Peace, peace!' when there is no peace?" (Jer. 6:14). We would do well to remember that we are not preaching a biblical gospel unless we are also giving a biblical gospel invitation.

RECEIVING CHRIST IN WHOLE

In the prologue of John's gospel is one of the most beautiful promises of salvation in the Scriptures: "But as many as received Him, to them He gave the right to become children of God, to those who believe in His name" (1:12). For good reason, this text has become one of the most frequently employed in modern-day evangelism. Many have used it rightly to bring multitudes into Christ's kingdom. However, many have wrongly used it to lead multitudes to a false assurance of salvation. For this reason, it is necessary for us to understand the text and its biblical application correctly before we endeavor to use it to bring people to Christ.

John immediately precedes this verse with a declaration of the Jews' almost full-scale rejection of the Messiah. It is briefly, yet powerfully, stated that Christ "came to His own [people, possession], and His own did not receive Him" (1:11). The word *receive* comes from the old, common Greek verb *paralambáno*, which means "to take to one's side," "to welcome." Jesus uses this word to describe the believer's welcome into the Father's heavenly mansion.[1]

Having dealt with the Jewish nation's failure to receive the Christ, John then proceeds to a glorious and universal promise for all: "But as many as received Him, to them He gave the right to become the children of God" (1:12). Adoption into the family of God with full rights and privileges of sonship is available to all—Jew and Gentile, king and servant, rich man and pauper, philosopher and imbecile, moralist and prostitute—even to all who receive Christ, to all who believe in His name.

We should not question that this is a universal invitation to eternal salvation and sonship. However, what *is* a matter of debate is how we are to appropriate this promise. What does it mean to receive Him? Is

---

1. John 14:3

this text a biblical basis for encouraging a seeker to open his heart and let Jesus in? Has a man received Christ because he agrees with the fundamental claims of the gospel, recognizes his need of forgiveness, and welcomes Jesus into his life through a prayer? These interpretive questions must be resolved.

There is nothing exceptional about the Greek word for "received" that would help us better understand what it means to receive Jesus. However, the context for the word does provide us with some insight. The first interpretive clue is found in the last phrase of the verse where John equates those who "received" Christ with those who "believe in His name." In the Scriptures, to believe is not limited to an intellectual understanding of certain facts or even to the acceptance of them. Instead, it is to trust in and rely upon the object of our faith to the degree that we base our actions upon it. Our faith or belief in Jesus Christ is not validated by the strength of our verbal confession or even by what we supposedly feel in our hearts; rather, it is proven true or false by the degree to which His person and will determine our actions and direct the full course of our lives. Thus, true belief involves an element of risk on the part of the believer because he is literally staking his life upon the claim that Jesus is "the Christ, the Son of the living God" (Matt. 16:16). As the apostle Paul wrote to the church in Corinth, if the claims of Christ are not true, then the genuine believer is "of all men most pitiable" because the entire course of his life has been founded upon a lie (1 Cor. 15:19). Therefore, to "receive Christ" is to trust or rely upon Him to such a degree that we stake both our temporal and eternal well-being on the truthfulness of His claims, and we direct the entire course of our lives according to His will.

The second interpretive clue is in the phrase "in His name." In the Scriptures, to believe in the name of God is to believe in the totality of His person or to believe in everything that He has revealed about Himself. The Scriptures leave no room for believing in one part of God's self-revelation and rejecting another, or receiving one aspect of His person without receiving the whole. The idea that one could enter into a covenant relationship with God by accepting Him in part is unbiblical. It is equally untenable to think that a person could "receive" Jesus as Savior at one stage in life and then receive Him as Lord and King later. To receive Jesus in a manner that results in salvation and sonship is to receive the whole of Him as prophet, priest, and king. Although the believer's faith in Christ as Savior and submission to Christ as Lord may be meager at first, it will be real, and through the continuing work of salvation, it will grow to maturity.

The third interpretive clue is found in the preceding verse, where the genuine believer's receiving of Christ stands in direct contrast with the Jewish nation's rejection of Him. Those of us far removed from the Jewish culture and religion of Jesus' day often forget that the Jews were not merely looking for a deliverer but also for a king. The Messiah was to be a son of David who sat upon the throne of David. He was to rule as an absolute sovereign. For this reason, when the Jews rejected Jesus as the Christ, they did not say, "We have no *savior* but Caesar!" Rather, they said, "We have no *king* but Caesar!" (John 19:15, emphasis added). Thus, the coming Messiah was not only going to extend an olive leaf of peace toward His people as savior, but He was also going to extend a royal scepter toward them as king. The Jews had no concept of a Messiah who would save them and yet not rule over them. If they "received Him" as deliverer, they would also welcome Him as king.

What was true for the Jewish nation in the time of Christ continues to be true today for both Jew and Gentile. To receive Christ is to receive the whole of Him and take Him in as Savior and Lord. For this reason, Isaiah prophesied concerning the Messiah, saying, "There shall be a root of Jesse; and He who shall rise to reign over the Gentiles, in Him the Gentiles shall hope" (Rom. 15:12). For this reason, we can properly say that the Christ in whom he has hoped will also rule the Gentile who has hoped in Christ for salvation. He is not only the king of the Jews but also the king of the believing Gentiles.

The following illustration shows a correct understanding of what it means to receive Christ as Savior and Lord. Imagine a walled city under the peril of destruction from an approaching army. While the enemy is still far off, a great king approaches the city gates and calls to the people within. He commands them to open the gates and turn over complete sovereignty to him. In return, he promises salvation from the approaching army. In one scenario, the people laugh him to scorn. Either they believe they have no need of a savior, or they do not believe that this one king can save them. In either case, the king turns away and the city is destroyed. In another scenario, the people recognize the king's power to save and are willing to receive him as savior, but they refuse to turn over their sovereignty to him. Again, the king turns away and the city is destroyed. In the last scenario, the people recognize the king's power to save and joyfully throw open the gates of the city to receive him as both savior and sovereign. The king enters the city, takes the throne, and delivers the people.

In a similar manner, we receive Christ into our lives. At the moment of conversion, we realize that we are in a desperate state from which we cannot save ourselves. In turn, we hear the call of Christ, the demands of His kingdom, and the promise of salvation. In response, we open our lives to Him and receive Him as Savior and Lord. We reject autonomy and acknowledge His sovereign rule over us. We denounce our own strength and merit and rely upon His power alone to save. Consequently, the evidence that we have truly received Him is that our submission to His lordship and our reliance upon His saving work deepens and becomes a greater and greater reality throughout the full course of our lives. This ongoing work of sanctification is guaranteed in the life of every believer. "For we are His workmanship," and "He who has begun a good work in [us] will complete it until the day of Jesus Christ" (Eph. 2:10; Phil. 1:6).

Modern-day evangelism does not often emphasize these truths. Instead, seekers are led to believe they can receive the benefits of Christ's salvation without submitting to the rule of His sovereignty. Furthermore, they often feel assured of their salvation because they prayed the sinner's prayer with sincerity, even though there is no evidence of a continuing work of sanctification in their lives. This is the malady of our time, leading to the deception and destruction of many people.

RECEIVING CHRIST AS OUR ALL

The receiving of Christ unto salvation not only concerns His sovereignty but also His supremacy. The gospel does not call us to receive Christ as an addition to our life, but rather as our life. Jesus Christ is not to be treated as an accessory to our lives in the same manner that a belt or pair of shoes might accessorize a certain outfit. It is the worst thing to tell sinners that they have a great life, a wonderful family, a beautiful home, and a great job, but they lack one thing to make it all complete—a personal relationship with Jesus Christ! Such language portrays Jesus as a cherry on top of an already great life. At best, it makes Him nothing more than a necessary or complementary addition. Such language degrades Christ to the point of blasphemy. It is foreign to the Scriptures and to those saints throughout the history of Christianity who best understood the supremacy of His person and the privilege of His gospel. In contrast, Puritan preacher and author John Flavel (1627–1691) speaks of Christ this way:

> O fair sun, and fair moon, and fair stars, and fair flowers, and fair roses, and fair lilies, and fair creatures! But, O ten thousand, thousand times fairer Lord Jesus! Alas, I wronged Him in making the comparison this way. O black sun and moon; but O fair Lord Jesus! O black flowers, and black lilies and roses; but O fair, fair, even fair Lord Jesus! O all fair things, black, deformed, and without beauty, when ye are set beside the fairest Lord Jesus! O black heaven, but O fair Christ! O black angels, but O surpassingly fair Lord Jesus.[2]

If we truly know Christ and we are honest ambassadors, we must throw off any language that would suggest there could be anything good in heaven or earth apart from Christ. Is it not true that "all things were made through Him, and without Him nothing was made that was made" (John 1:3)? Is it not true that a Christless life is vanity and less than nothing?[3] Is it not true that no good thing dwells in us apart from Christ, and that all our righteous deeds are as filthy rags?[4] Therefore, how dare we even suppose or suggest that fallen people need Christ only as a complement to what they already are or have already achieved by their own strength or virtue? We would do better to tell the sinner this: "Your life is a useless vanity.[5] From the sole of your foot to the top of your head, there is nothing sound in you.[6] You say, 'I am rich, have become wealthy, and have need of nothing.' Yet you do not know that you are 'wretched, miserable, poor, blind, and naked.'[7] Your family is flesh whose duration on this earth will be as a vapor.[8] You have led them to neglect their God and made them like chaff that the wind drives away.[9] Your material achievements will be a testimony against you on the day of judgment, and your works will burn in the fire.[10] Your money will not avail you,

---

2. John Flavel, "Epistle Dedicatory," in *The Works of John Flavel* (London: Banner of Truth, 1968), 1: xix–xx.

3. Ecclesiastes 1:2

4. Isaiah 64:6; Romans 7:18

5. Romans 3:12

6. Isaiah 1:6

7. Revelation 3:17

8. James 4:14

9. Psalm 1:4

10. 1 Corinthians 3:11–15

for the redemption of a soul is costly.[11] And what does it profit you if you have gained the whole world and yet forfeit your soul?[12] Repent and turn to Christ in faith. Count all lost, and consider your achievements as rubbish that you might gain Christ and be found in Him!"[13]

The modern-day evangelical is most likely to respond to this straightforwardness with the words, "This is a hard saying; who can understand it?" (John 6:60). The church-growth expert and the missionary on the cutting edge of contextualization in missions will most likely reject these hard words, arguing that modern people are too fragile and fractured of heart to bear such a denunciation. Such language, though biblical, was meant for another time when people were more robust in their psyche and surer of their self-worth. However, nothing could be more preposterous. It is the task of the gospel preacher to convince people that they are nothing and that they have nothing apart from Christ! The true gospel message ransacks the soul and carries off every spoil. It leaves the heart with nothing so that Christ may enter in as everything! If a person saw everything in comparison to Christ, as Flavel did, wouldn't his heart be much improved? It is not wrong to preach a gospel that takes everything away from a person, yet leaves him with Christ alone. Is Christ not enough? Is He not more than the entire world?

As Christians and ministers of the gospel, we must preach Christ as altogether lovely and to be esteemed above all the riches of this world and the next. We must hold Him up in stark contrast to the shadows and types of this lower world. However, to proclaim Christ in this way, we must know Him in this way! Yet only those who tarry with Him and seek Him in the Word of God and prayer obtain such knowledge. If we would only spend more time with Him, we would know Him better and proclaim Him with more power. Then our joy and zeal would outshine and shame those with lesser gods.

RECEIVING CHRIST AS OUR SUSTENANCE

In the synagogue in Capernaum, Jesus declared to the Jews, "I am the bread of life," and, "Most assuredly, I say to you, unless you eat the flesh of the Son of Man and drink His blood, you have no life in you" (John

---

11. Psalm 49:7–9
12. Mark 8:36–37
13. Philippians 3:8–9

6:48, 53). Although there are numerous truths in these statements, we will briefly consider only one of them: to receive Jesus is to receive Him as the very sustenance and source of life. He is not something that we merely add to our life to make it complete or something that aids us in achieving life to its fullest, but He is our life, our food and drink, the very sap of life flowing from the vine to the branches.[14]

Although the new convert only meagerly comprehends this truth, and it is barely a reality in his life, the God who began a good work in him will see to its growth.[15] As the believer continues on his Christian pilgrimage, the things of this world will grow strangely dim in the light of Christ's glory and grace.[16] The believer will find that self-sufficiency and self-satisfaction are eclipsed by his increasing dependence upon Christ and greater satisfaction in Him. Through the work of sanctification, the arm of the flesh will gradually hang limp for lack of use, and the believer will abandon the broken cisterns he has dug by his own hands for the all-satisfying fountain of living waters that has opened up in the house of David.[17]

That we are to receive Christ as the source and sustenance of our life leads us to two important applications. First, Christ is not merely a course in the meal, but He is the meal in its entirety: our all-sufficient source of everything pertaining to life and godliness.[18] As the apostle Paul wrote to the church in Corinth, Christ becomes to us "wisdom from God—and righteousness and sanctification and redemption," so that we no longer boast in self or religious performance but in the Lord and His work on our behalf (1 Cor. 1:30–31). To receive Christ is to renounce self-sufficiency, to put away all former trophies, and to refuse all present and future accolades. It is to bear joyfully one title alone throughout all of eternity: "recipient of grace."

To be truly Christian is to recognize that every good and perfect gift comes from above through the person and work of Jesus Christ.[19] It is to denounce any suggestion of self-generated worth or merit and joyfully and publicly to confess that any good, personal attainment or calculable worth in us is from Christ alone. It is to live as dependent upon Him as the

---

14. John 15:1–6; Colossians 3:4
15. Philippians 1:6
16. Helen H. Lemmel, "Turn Your Eyes upon Jesus," refrain.
17. Jeremiah 2:13; Zechariah 13:1
18. 2 Peter 1:3
19. James 1:17

air we breathe and the water and food that sustain our flesh. It is to be so satisfied in Him that we no longer spend our money for what is not bread, and our wages for what does not satisfy.[20] It is to fix our place at Christ's table and to no longer search out complementary dishes or worldly substitutes. We have tasted and seen that the Lord is good![21] What are the leeks and onions of Egypt compared to the manna of Christ?[22]

The second application of the truth that Christ is the believer's sustenance is that the feast is not a once-for-all meal confined to the moment of conversion and never to be repeated but rather a continual feast throughout the entirety of the believer's life. Conversion is simply the beginning of a lifelong, eternal meal that the Holy Spirit grants in ever-increasing measure to the ever-maturing Christian. One of the great sins of contemporary evangelicalism is that it treats salvation as a one-time past event with little consideration of its ongoing nature in the present and future. We should remember that ongoing or lifelong sanctification is the evidence of once-for-all conversion. In a similar manner, the Christian's continual feeding on Christ is evidence he has experienced an initial sitting-down at His table. Jesus is not a ticket to heaven that a person purchases with a prayer, then hides in a pocket until he finally withdraws it at the moment of death to obtain entrance into heaven. Salvation is not real if it is considered a one-time transaction that supposedly seals the fate of those who have prayed the sinner's prayer.

At conversion, the sinner tastes and sees that the Lord is good.[23] However, his palate is not refined. The residue of this world still rots in his belly, and his ability to savor true food is dulled. The hearty meat of Christ is too strong for him, and he must take only milk.[24] As the writer of Hebrews teaches us, "Everyone…is unskilled in the word of righteousness, for he is a babe" (Heb. 5:13). However, God has promised that the new Christian will not remain in that state but will grow into the full stature of a man. Thus, God commands and enables him to lay aside the deadly diet of this present age and, like a newborn babe, long for the pure milk of the word, so that by it he may grow in respect to salvation.[25]

---

20. Isaiah 55:2
21. Psalm 34:8
22. Numbers 11:5
23. Psalm 34:8
24. Hebrews 5:12
25. 1 Peter 2:1–3

Gradually, through divine training, the renewing of the mind, and the grace supplied to overcome, the Holy Spirit trains the believer's senses to discern good and evil, to shun the world's menu, and to desire Christ alone.[26] The aftertaste of rotten flesh is gradually purged from him, and his spiritual senses are refined. He not only forgets the food of Egypt, but he comes to loathe it. Like Mephibosheth, he becomes accustomed to the king's table, and not only does he no longer desire the common victuals of this world, but he disdains them.[27]

Before we close this brief discussion, it is important to reiterate that at conversion, no one fully comprehends what it means to receive Christ, to be completely dependent upon Him, or to long for Him alone. Though we welcome Him by the Spirit's urging and enabling, our understanding is mixed with error, our motives are mingled with selfish desires, and our hearts are divided between competing loyalties. Even after decades of God's work of sanctification in our lives, these maladies are never completely eradicated. Though our spiritual state is much improved, our dependence upon Christ deepened, and our desire for Him increased, we are still not wholly His. A perfect heart remains beyond our reach until we are glorified in His presence.

This is why it would be terribly wrong to demand a mature comprehension and devotion from a new convert when the most mature saint struggles to comprehend and appreciate the same. Although sanctification is the real proof of justification, and a continual receiving of Christ is evidence of having received Him unto salvation, we must be careful that we do not steal assurance from the saints by making perfection the evidence of faith or unblemished devotion the proof of salvation. We will always be struggling to apprehend that for which we were apprehended: conformity to Jesus Christ.[28] The evidence of salvation is not having attained the goal, but rather a sincere struggle to grow in holiness and a gradual progress in the things of God. Those who have truly received Christ show evidence of growing into a fuller understanding of Him as He becomes a greater and greater reality in their life. Those who have supposedly received Him yet never grow into a greater reality of what that means demonstrate little proof of genuine conversion.

---

26. Hebrews 5:14
27. 2 Samuel 9:6–7
28. Philippians 3:12–14

CHAPTER FIVE

Christis at Heart's Door

Behold, I stand at the door and knock. If anyone hears My voice and opens the door, I will come in to him and dine with him, and he with Me.
—Revelation 3:20

"Christ at Heart's Door" by Sallman Warner is a religious painting that is well recognized by both evangelicals and Roman Catholics.[1] The artist based his painting on Christ's call to the church of Laodicea in Revelation 3:20: "Behold, I stand at the door and knock. If anyone hears My voice and opens the door, I will come in to him and dine with him, and he with Me."

According to the artist's interpretation of the text, Christ is knocking upon the door of the human heart and asking to come in. What is most noticeable is the absence of any outside doorknob or latch, which was not an oversight on the part of the artist. Rather, he intended to illustrate that the human heart can be opened only from within. The always gracious Christ will not pry open the door or force His way inside. God is willing to save, but it is up to a person to open his heart and allow Him entrance. Prints of this work hang in many large cathedrals and tiny chapels throughout the Western world. Numerous evangelistic sermons, tracts, and books reference this painting. It has become an important hallmark of the evangelistic invitation.

A FAULTY INTERPRETATION

We can hardly exaggerate the power of any form of media. Most people do not base their idea of history on primary resources but rather on

1. Sallman Warner (1892–1968) was a Christian painter from Chicago. His work is based on British painter William Holman Hunt's previous work "The Light of the World," completed in 1853.

media's interpretation of that event through a still-life painting, a novel, or a major motion picture. Cecil B. DeMille's 1956 movie *The Ten Commandments* is a good illustration of this. Many people's understanding of Israel's exodus from Egypt is based more on this popular film than the Scriptures.

Similarly, it seems many who preach evangelistic sermons on Revelation 3:20 base them more on Warner's painting than on a serious consideration of the text. Thus, preachers tell people that Christ is knocking on the door of their heart, and they alone have the power to open the door by inviting Him in through prayer. If a person does pray and is confident he is sincere, he is assured that Christ has come into his heart and saved him. He is told that he should stand on this truth by faith and not trust in his feelings or emotions. Those who counsel new converts often confront their doubts with the following reasoning:

1. Christ promised to come into your heart if you open the door.

2. You have opened the door by faith and prayer.

3. Christ always keeps His promises, and, therefore, He has come into your heart. If He has not, then He is a liar.

4. However, we know that Christ does not lie. Therefore, we know that your salvation is secure.

Because of this logic, numerous individuals believe they are saved, even though they show little evidence of change in their lives. They do not show the slightest devotion to Christ in their daily lives, and they are without any of the outward markings of true Christianity. How can we explain this? The text is not at fault; rather, it is the popular interpretation and application of it.

When we look at Revelation 3:20 in its context, we see something quite different from that set before us in modern-day evangelism. First, Christ is not knocking on the door of the sinner's heart, but on the door of the church of Laodicea. Second, He is not asking people to invite Him into some deep recess of their heart through praying a prayer. Instead, He is reproving a group of people who congregate in His name and commanding them to repent of their apathy toward Him (they are lukewarm), their spiritual blindness (they cannot see that they are wretched, miserable, poor, blind, and naked), and their materialism and pride (they say they are rich and have become wealthy and have need of nothing).[2] Third, He is not calling men to faith in the gospel or promising eternal life to a group of unbelieving seekers. Rather, He is promising restored fellowship and eternal reward to those individuals in the church who hear His voice and renew their relationship with Him through genuine repentance.

A DANGEROUS CONTRADICTION

That the immediate context and purpose of Revelation 3:20 has little to do with evangelism ought to raise some red flags. This is particularly true when we realize that Scripture nowhere commands people to respond to the gospel message by opening their hearts and asking Jesus in. Instead, Scripture commands people to repent of their sins and trust in Christ.[3]

It is also interesting that this text has become the basis for most contemporary evangelistic methodologies and one of the Scriptures most employed in actual evangelism, even though it has little to do with evangelism. At the same time, Acts 16:14, which provides a biblical description of apostolic evangelism and the work of God in salvation, is almost entirely ignored: "Now a certain woman named Lydia heard us. She was a seller of purple from the city of Thyatira, who worshiped God. The Lord opened her heart to heed the things spoken by Paul."

Many preachers use Revelation 3:20 as a basis for exhorting people to open their hearts' door to Christ and to illustrate that the handle to the human heart is on the inside. This is to demonstrate that God cannot or will not open it from without, and humans alone possess the power to do so. Like in Warner's painting, Christ waits helplessly on the outside, pleading to be granted entrance. The text, then, is used to illustrate a doctrine it does not teach and to validate an evangelistic methodology that is found nowhere in Scripture.

Furthermore, the contemporary interpretation and use of Revelation 3:20 is a direct contradiction of the clear teaching of Acts 16:14, where the Scriptures declare clearly that God opened Lydia's heart to respond to the things Paul spoke. There, the word *open* is translated from the Greek word *dianoígo*,[4] which renowned Greek scholar A. T. Robertson defines as "to open up wide or completely like both sides of a

---

2. Revelation 3:16–17
3. Mark 1:15; Luke 24:46–47; Acts 16:30–31; 17:30
4. From the Greek prefix *día* (two, asunder, through) and the verb *anoígo* (to open).

folding door."[5] Greek lexicologist Joseph Henry Thayer gives it a similar meaning: "to open by dividing or drawing asunder, to open thoroughly.[6] Elsewhere in his writings, Luke uses the same word to describe the firstborn opening his mother's womb,[7] Jesus opening the disciples' minds to understand the Scriptures,[8] and God opening the heavens to reveal Jesus standing at His right hand.[9] These events are not passive; rather, they demonstrate both action and power, the first on the child's part and the latter two on God's part.

A Proper Use
Contemporary evangelism dangerously misuses Revelation 3:20, but the text does have valid use as a gospel invitation if sound theology and a proper understanding of genuine conversion accompany it. Although most serious scholars immediately point out that Christ is addressing an apathetic, self-satisfied, and self-deluded congregation, they also admit that the text can provide an illustration of Christ's patience with the sinner and His enduring offer of fellowship. Seen in a proper light, we can apply Revelation 3:20 in the following manner.

"Behold, I Stand at the Door and Knock…"
This text illustrates the truth that there is a universal call of the gospel, and no Christian should ever waver on that. Throughout the Scriptures, God has made it abundantly clear that He does not take pleasure in the death of the wicked, but rather he should turn from his ways and live.[10] Therefore, we are responsible to offer the gospel of Jesus Christ to every creature under heaven and to call all people everywhere to repentance and faith.[11] We are to do so fervently and consistently until the Lord's return. It should be our magnificent obsession to offer the gospel to every person of our generation without exception, and, in doing so, we should humbly advise our hearers that Christ has both visited and called them through the message that we have preached.

---

5. Robertson, *Word Pictures*, 3:252.
6. Thayer, *Greek-English Lexicon*, 140.
7. Luke 2:23
8. Luke 24:45
9. Acts 7:56
10. Ezekiel 18:23
11. Mark 16:15; Acts 17:30

Second, we learn from this text that God's call to the sinner is both patient and enduring. He is a compassionate and gracious God—slow to anger and abounding in lovingkindness and truth.[12] Therefore, He calls out to even the most hardened sinner, and He waits upon those who have shunned His mercies throughout the full course of their lives. Isaiah beautifully and powerfully illustrates God's longsuffering in his writings:

> I said, "Here I am, here I am,"
> To a nation that was not called by My name.
> I have stretched out My hands all day long to a rebellious people,
> Who walk in a way that is not good,
> According to their own thoughts;
> A people who provoke Me to anger continually to My face (65:1–3).

The preacher should make much of God's longsuffering toward sinners because it is God's kindness, tolerance, and patience that lead people to repentance.[13] However, the preacher is obliged to warn the sinner of a day known only to God when the call of salvation will end, and judgment will be all that remains.

"If Anyone Hears My Voice and Opens the Door..."
The awesome truth revealed in this phrase is that God calls people to respond to the gospel message. Any sort of preaching that does not demand a response from people is unbalanced at best and heretical at worst. The evangelist has not done his job if he merely proclaims the message and then leaves the hearer without a sense of urgency, without a sense that he is undone until he has properly responded to the gospel's demands. This is clear from the examples left to us in the Scriptures by the Lord and His apostles. From the beginning of His ministry, Jesus commanded people to respond to the gospel with repentance and faith.[14] On Pentecost, Peter strongly exhorted his listeners to action, saying, "Be saved from this perverse generation" (Acts 2:40). The apostle Paul both persuaded and implored sinners on behalf of Christ to be reconciled to God.[15] It is from him that we read one of Scripture's most powerful exhortations to sinners: "Behold, now is the accepted time; behold, now is the day of salvation" (2 Cor. 6:2).

---

12. Exodus 34:6
13. Romans 2:4
14. Mark 1:15
15. 2 Corinthians 5:11, 20

The gospel clearly and unashamedly demands a response from the one who hears it. However, that response is not confined to repeating a prayer on the back of a gospel tract in private or at the end of an evangelistic message. The full counsel of Scripture is that sinners are to respond by opening their lives to the saving work and sovereign rule of Christ. Scripture calls upon them to repent of their sins, to turn from all forms of autonomy or self-government, and to confess Jesus as Lord.[16] Scripture commands them to shun all hope of salvation through the arm of their own flesh and throw themselves by faith upon the mercies of God in Christ. To help us understand the significance of hearing Christ's voice and opening the door of our lives to Him, we must consider the following texts from the gospel of John:

> Most assuredly, I say to you, the hour is coming, and now is, when the dead will hear the voice of the Son of God; and those who hear will live (5:25).

> My sheep hear My voice, and I know them, and they follow Me (10:27).

In the first text, Christ speaks of salvation as a resurrection of the spiritually dead. It is a supernatural and miraculous work whereby He changes the very heart of the sinner and infuses him with spiritual life. By the magnificent and limitless power of Christ, the new convert is raised from the dead as a new creation, created in Christ Jesus to walk in the good works that God prepared for him before the very foundations of the world.[17] It is a spiritual resurrection that is no less miraculous or life changing than the raising of Lazarus at Christ's command. Therefore, it would be absurd to think that a person could truly hear Christ's voice and experience such a powerful work of God and yet be unchanged by the event. As John 5:25 teaches us, "Those who hear *will* live" (emphasis added). Consequently, they will also "walk in newness of life" (Rom. 6:4).

In the second text from John's gospel, we see that one of the characteristics of those who have truly heard Christ's voice and opened their lives to Him is that they continue to follow Him. It is preposterous to think and heretical to teach that a person could hear Christ's voice and be raised from spiritual death, yet experience no enduring effects of such an event in his life. Likewise, it is contrary to John 10:27 to believe that

---

16. Romans 10:9–10
17. 2 Corinthians 5:17; Ephesian 2:10

a person could open his life to Christ just long enough to receive salvation and then reclose himself so that he might live a life of self-autonomy without the slightest regard for his Savior. We would do well to remember that the Hebrew idea of *hearing* includes not only the act of listening but also the act of obeying.

We must again set forth a simple truth of the gospel: people are saved by grace alone, through faith alone; salvation is a gift of God, separate from all human merit and excluding all boasting in the flesh.[18] However, it is also by a supernatural work of the Spirit that a person becomes a new creature and God's workmanship. Such a truth guarantees that the person who has heard and opened his life to God's salvation will progress in personal sanctification and conformity to Christ. It is not because of the strength of the convert's will, but because of the power and faithfulness of the God who saves. He who began a good work in that person will finish it.[19]

"…I Will Come into Him…"

One of the greatest and most beloved realities of the new covenant is that Christ indwells His people. He is truly our Immanuel until the end of the age.[20] It is important to state that when the Scripture refers to Christ's indwelling of the believer, it is neither speaking poetically nor metaphorically but rather pointing to a reality that is true for every child of God. In His letter to the church in Colossae, the apostle Paul refers to Christ within us as the very foundation of the believer's hope for future glory.[21] The indwelling of Christ through the Spirit, producing both inward spiritual life and outward discernible transformation, assures the believer that he belongs to Christ and has good reason to hope in the final glory yet to come. Thus, the indwelling of Christ through the Spirit is not passive, but energetic.[22] It is not secret or limited to some mystical or subjective impression; rather, it is a discernible or noticeable reality.

---

18. Ephesians 2:8–9

19. Philippians 1:6

20. Isaiah 7:14; Matthew 1:23; 28:20

21. Colossians 1:27. A. T. Robertson writes, "He is addressing Gentiles, but the idea of 'in' here is 'in,' not 'among.' It is the personal experience and presence of Christ in the individual life of all believers that Paul has in mind, the indwelling Christ in the heart as in Ephesians 3:17. He constitutes also the hope of glory for he is the *shekina* of God. Christ is our hope now (1 Timothy 1:1) and of the consummation that will come (Romans 8:18)." *Word Pictures*, 4:485.

22. William Hendriksen, *New Testament Commentary: Exposition of Colossians and Philemon* (Grand Rapids: Baker, 1964), 91.

Christ promises to come into all who receive Him by faith, yet we must reiterate that the evidence of faith, the proof that we have received Him, will be the active working of Christ in us to conform us to His image, a gradual and yet enduring transformation of the one confessing His name. In the gospel of John is a text that has great bearing on what it means for Christ to indwell the believer: "Jesus answered and said to him, 'If anyone loves Me, he will keep My word; and My Father will love him, and We will come to him and make Our home with him'" (14:23).

Jesus is not teaching that His indwelling of the believer is based upon the magnitude of the believer's love toward Him or the thoroughness of the believer's obedience. Love for Christ and the keeping of His Word does not procure His indwelling, but rather they demonstrate its reality. We know we have been born again and indwelt by Christ through the Spirit because we have a love for Him that was previously nonexistent, and we demonstrate a new relationship with His Word that is marked by increasing obedience to it.

This biblical teaching stands in stark contrast to the popular idea that people can stand firm upon the hope of their salvation simply because they once prayed and asked Jesus to come into their hearts. Even though they experience no inward feeling or outward evidence that Christ has indwelt them, they must stand firm simply because He has truly promised and they have sincerely asked. This treats the indwelling of Christ as a passive, powerless, and indiscernible reality. Salvation becomes nothing more than a ticket to heaven with no expectation that it will have a discernible effect upon a person's character or relationship with God.

However popular this interpretation may be, it has no foundation in Scripture. Although a person may experience increased assurance when he considers his conversion experience, such a consideration is not the only factor in determining the validity of his profession of faith in Christ. There are other important and indispensable factors, such as God's continuing work in the believer's life producing sanctification: a deepening of repentance, a growing in faith, a greater appreciation for Christ, and a more thorough submission to His will.

"...And Dine with Him, and He with Me"
One of the greatest promises of the gospel is fellowship with Christ, yet this seems to have taken a back seat to a more desirable benefit: the

sinner's self-preservation. People are encouraged to ask Jesus to come into their heart because they have the promise of a better life in this world, and they avoid eternal destruction in the next. Although these promises are valid, when we give them a higher priority than the promise of fellowship with Christ, they distort the gospel. It is a contradiction to the meaning of eternal life as Jesus saw it: "And this is eternal life, that they may know You, the only true God, and Jesus Christ whom You have sent" (John 17:3).

The devil discerned correctly when he stated that a man would do almost anything to save his own skin.[23] He will pray a prayer, attend church, involve himself in religious service, and even offer himself as a martyr. However, radically transforming a depraved human being so he might esteem Christ and desire fellowship with Him requires a supernatural work of the Spirit of God. The offer of a better life or eternal bliss will draw a great many carnal people, but the offer of fellowship with Christ will draw no one except those the Spirit of God draws: "No one can come to Me unless the Father who sent Me draws him; and I will raise him up at the last day" (John 6:44).

As Christians and ministers of the gospel, we must remember two important truths as we use Revelation 3:20 to share Christ with others. First, we must purpose to make much of Christ and to display His worth to our hearers so that they might desire His fellowship above all. Although there are countless benefits of the gospel that we should make known, we must proclaim Christ as the chief of all these benefits, and as more valuable than the combined worth of them. In fact, we should endeavor to show the sinner that in light of Christ, all other benefits are of little worth or consequence.

What can the preacher offer in comparison to Christ? Should we leave aside this exalted theme and speak of lesser things in order to attract carnal people who would rather eat at a swine's trough than dine at the Lord's Table? If we make the beauty of Christ and the glory of His gospel our main theme, we may draw fewer people, but those who do come will not come in vain. By the Spirit of God, they will come because of Christ, and they will stay because of Christ. Though every promise of earthly joy and prosperity seems to fail them, they will hold the course because they

---

23. "So Satan answered the Lord and said, 'Skin for skin! Yes, all that a man has he will give for his life'" (Job 2:4).

have caught one glimpse of the glorious Christ, and they have counted everything else as rubbish in comparison.[24]

Second, we must use this beloved text to show that the evidence that a person has opened the door to Christ or experienced true conversion is that he continues in fellowship with Christ. Jesus promised, "I will come into him and dine with him, and he with Me." Here, Jesus is teaching a vital truth that the result of His indwelling of the new believer will be the beginning and continuation of a real and enduring fellowship between Himself and that person. This is one of the marks of true conversion. We know or have assurance that Christ has both saved and indwelt us because of our mutual fellowship: He dines with us, and we with Him.

It is extremely important to note that this promise of abiding fellowship is not stated as a mere possibility but as a certain reality—as something that will happen in the life of every true believer. It is very similar to one of the most beautiful Old Testament promises regarding the new covenant: "For this is the covenant that I will make with the house of Israel after those days, says the Lord: I will put My laws in their mind and write them on their hearts; and I will be their God, and they shall be My people."[25]

This covenant promise speaks of a time now fulfilled when God would create for Himself a people reconciled by the atoning death of the Messiah and regenerated by the Holy Spirit. Because of His supernatural work on their behalf, He would be their God and they would be His people. This is not wishful thinking on the part of a hopeful God, but rather an immutable decree from an all-sovereign God. Not only does He pledge His enduring faithfulness to this renewed people, but He also promises to work in them in such a way that they will respond appropriately. They will be His people.

In Revelation 3:20, we see something of the same certainty. Christ not only promises that He will continue in fellowship with the true convert but that His indwelling of that person will ensure that he will respond in kind. This does not mean that the believer will always hold the course without failure or that his devotion to Christ will never grow lukewarm. However, it does mean that the believer's life will be marked by a real and discernible fellowship with Christ. He will not found his assurance of salvation merely

---

24. Philippians 3:7–8
25. Jeremiah 24:7; 31:33; 32:38; Hebrews 8:10

upon a prayer he prayed long ago that he believed was sincere but upon an enduring and mutual relationship with the living Christ.

LOOK WHO'S COMING TO DINNER

Before we set aside this subject and move on, we must say one last thing. Many of the problems associated with using Revelation 3:20 as a means of evangelism would be cleared up if we simply understood and correctly proclaimed who it is that is knocking at the door. He is not the outcast Christ, begging for scraps of devotion. He is the Lord of glory! What does He need with humans? He sits enthroned in heaven, and the earth is His footstool.[26] Human hands do not serve Him, as though He needed anything, for He Himself gives to all people life and breath and all things.[27] If He were hungry, He would not tell it to men, for the whole world is His and all it contains.[28] Furthermore, if a person sins or multiplies his transgression, what does it accomplish against God? In addition, if a man is righteous, what does it benefit Him?[29] A. W. Tozer was right: "Were all human beings suddenly to become blind, still the sun would shine by day and the stars by night, for these owe nothing to the millions who benefit from their light. So, were every man on earth to become atheist, it could not affect God in any way. He is what He is in Himself without regard to any other. To believe in Him adds nothing to His perfections; to doubt Him takes nothing away."[30]

Thus, Christ knocks on the door of the human heart as a gracious Lord we should revere and honor, and not as a beggarly outcast we should pity. When He enters the human heart, He makes all the conditions and demands. He does not bend His will to the whims of people but demands the allegiance of their entire person. This is why Christ teaches us in the Beatitudes, "Blessed are the pure in heart" (Matt. 5:8). Blessed are those whose hearts are unalloyed and without mixed or competing loyalties, for they shall see God.

For the sake of illustration, let's say that Christ is knocking on the door of a human heart. He offers a person great promises of healing,

---

26. Isaiah 66:1
27. Acts 17:25
28. Psalm 50:12
29. Job 35:6–7
30. A. W. Tozer, *The Knowledge of the Holy* (New York: Harper & Row, 1961), 40.

peace, and eternal life. Then, on hearing the benefits of such a salvation, the person reaches for the handle of the door and is ready to open. However, before he moves the latch, Christ speaks to him a word of warning: "If you open the door, I will come in and fulfill every promise I have made to you, but I will come as Lord, and My will is law. All that you are and all that you have is mine to do with according to My good will and purpose. You will be My servant, and I will be your Lord. I will teach you, test you, discipline you, and take from you everything that does not please Me. I will take mastery of your life and conform you to My image. Be forewarned! The moment you open the door to Me, you will close the door to everything else. A yes to Me is a no to the world, and to gain Me is to lose the world." A denial of such a gospel call is a denial of everything that Jesus Christ ever taught about the radical and demanding nature of true conversion and discipleship.

PART TWO

New Hearts and the Nature of True Conversion

Therefore say to the house of Israel, "Thus says the Lord GOD: 'I do not do this for your sake, O house of Israel, but for My holy name's sake, which you have profaned among the nations wherever you went. And I will sanctify My great name, which has been profaned among the nations, which you have profaned in their midst; and the nations shall know that I am the LORD,' says the Lord GOD, 'when I am hallowed in you before their eyes. For I will take you from among the nations, gather you out of all countries, and bring you into your own land. Then I will sprinkle clean water on you, and you shall be clean; I will cleanse you from all your filthiness and from all your idols. I will give you a new heart and put a new spirit within you; I will take the heart of stone out of your flesh and give you a heart of flesh. I will put My Spirit within you and cause you to walk in My statutes, and you will keep My judgments and do them. Then you shall dwell in the land that I gave to your fathers; you shall be My people, and I will be your God.'"

—Ezekiel 36:22–28

CHAPTER SIX

The Great Motive and End of Salvation

Therefore say to the house of Israel, "Thus says the Lord GOD: 'I do not do this for your sake, O house of Israel, but for My holy name's sake, which you have profaned among the nations wherever you went. And I will sanctify My great name, which has been profaned among the nations, which you have profaned in their midst; and the nations shall know that I am the LORD," says the Lord GOD, "when I am hallowed in you before their eyes.'"

—Ezekiel 36:22–23

Among the most important questions in the Christian religion are these: What could ever move a just and holy God to do good to evil people and work for their redemption? How can He be a friend of sinners when His eyes are too pure to behold evil?[1] Shall not the Judge of all the earth do right?[2]

Anyone who has seriously considered theology proper (i.e., the person and attributes of God) and the radical depravity of fallen humanity must immediately recognize that there is no affinity between the character and deeds of God and those of humans. God is good, just, and loving. Fallen humanity is evil, unrighteous, self-absorbed, and loveless. If such a low view of man is shocking to us, we should realize that the Scriptures are even more straightforward in their denunciation of humanity:

[Men are] filled with all unrighteousness, sexual immorality, wickedness, covetousness, maliciousness; full of envy, murder, strife, deceit, evil-mindedness; they are whisperers, backbiters, haters of God, violent, proud, boasters, inventors of evil things, disobedient

---

1. Habakkuk 1:13
2. Genesis 18:25

to parents, undiscerning, untrustworthy, unloving, unforgiving, unmerciful (Rom. 1:29–31).

> As it is written:
> "There is none righteous, no, not one;
> There is none who understands;
> There is none who seeks after God.
> They have all turned aside;
> They have together become unprofitable;
> There is none who does good, no, not one."
> "Their throat is an open tomb;
> With their tongues they have practiced deceit";
> "The poison of asps is under their lips";
> "Whose mouth is full of cursing and bitterness."
> "Their feet are swift to shed blood;
> Destruction and misery are in their ways;
> And the way of peace they have not known."
> "There is no fear of God before their eyes" (Rom. 3:10–18).

In light of Scripture's assessment of fallen man, the biblically trained mind does not ask how God can set Himself against men, condemn them, or even consign them to eternal separation. Rather, he asks how God can love men, justify them, and bring them into an intimate relationship with Himself without casting doubt upon His own virtue or integrity. After all, a person brings his morality into question by the relationships he indulges and the company he keeps.

The following illustrates the problem. A person can be judged evil because of his evil deeds. For example, Hitler has gone down in history as the epitome of human evil because of his atrocious crimes against humanity. However, a person who has not committed such deeds can still be considered evil because of his association with those who have. For example, a man who has not committed the atrocities of Hitler, but knows about them and still considers Hitler to be a friend and seeks to save him from the consequences of those atrocities would be considered evil. Although he would be innocent of any direct involvement with evil deeds, he demonstrates his evil by his association and friendship with the one who has committed them.

Why, then, would a holy and just God who hates evil and is repulsed by it be moved to seek a relationship with evil people and save them from the consequences of their sin? Before we consider the Scripture's answer, we must debunk a popular and blasphemous contemporary opinion: that God was moved to save humanity out of some divine need or longing for relationship.

It is distressing that so many have fallen so far that they can no longer see when an opinion is a direct contradiction of the Scriptures and historical Christian thought. One of the most important and encouraging doctrines regarding the attributes of God is His self-sufficiency. He has no need of anything; least of all does He need a relationship with man. Christianity in the West has exalted the worth of man beyond measure so that it now practically holds humanity above God as the end of all things and possessing a value beyond all estimation. We have convinced ourselves that heaven would not be heaven without us, and God would not be complete if humanity were lost. However, the Scriptures calculate the total worth of the nations as "a drop in a bucket" and "as the small dust on the scales" (Isa. 40:15). To answer the notion that God has a need that only man can meet, the apostle Paul puts forth the following rebuttal: "God, who made the world and everything in it, since He is Lord of heaven and earth, does not dwell in temples made with hands" (Acts 17:24).

God has no lack and therefore no need for anything or anyone outside of Himself to maintain or enhance His existence. Furthermore, God has no need of relationship, since the Father, Son, and Spirit have existed in perfect fellowship with one another throughout eternity. The infinitely bountiful God did not create the world out of some divine need but out of His superabundance.

THE LOVE OF GOD

We will now turn to the Scriptures to answer the question before us: What moved God to save us? The first answer we will consider is in 1 John 4:8. In one sense, this answer should come as no surprise to the Christian, and yet in another sense, it should always surprise and astonish him: "God is love." God loved fallen humanity because God *is* love. This simple statement does not merely teach that God *loves*, though that in itself is an extraordinary truth, but that He *is* love—that the love of God is much more than a decision, disposition, or work. It is an *attribute* of God, a part of His very being or nature. Because of who He is, He freely and selflessly gives Himself to others for their benefit or good. Thus, God's love toward people is the result of who He *is* and has nothing to do with some worth or merit found in the objects of His love. He did not save people because of them, but in spite of them. God's love flows out from Him by His own virtue and will. Some virtue or merit—evident or latent, inherent or derived—in the character or deeds of man does not draw it out of Him. The logic is simple: God saves evil men because He loves them, and He loves them because He *is* love.

This truth of the undeserved and unconditional love of God is wonderfully illustrated in Deuteronomy, where God explains the basis or motivation for His choosing Israel. Moses reminds the people, "The LORD did not set His love on you nor choose you because you were more in number than any other people, for you were the least of all peoples; but because the LORD loves you" (7:7–8).

Israel asks, "Why have you loved me?" and God replies, "I loved you because I loved you." Thus, God's love for Israel and for all of fallen humanity has nothing to do with who they are or what they have done; rather, it has everything to do with who God is and what He has determined. God loves sinful and fallen people because He is love, and He has determined to set His love upon them.

The truth of God's love in spite of fallen humanity's complete lack of merit is further illustrated in the book of Ezekiel. There, God describes the miserable, even repulsive, nature of Israel—and all of us—prior to His redemptive work in our lives:

> Thus says the Lord God to Jerusalem: "Your birth and your nativity are from the land of Canaan; your father was an Amorite and your mother a Hittite. As for your nativity, on the day you were born your navel cord was not cut, nor were you washed in water to cleanse you; you were not rubbed with salt nor wrapped in swaddling cloths. No eye pitied you, to do any of these things for you, to have compassion on you; but you were thrown out into the open field, when you yourself were loathed on the day you were born.
>
> And when I passed by you and saw you struggling in your own blood, I said to you in your blood, "Live!" Yes, I said to you in your blood, "Live!" (Ezek. 16:3–6).

In this text, God describes the people of Israel—and all of fallen humanity—as a child of shameful lineage and ignoble birth: born of an enemy race, filthy and aborted, abandoned in an open field, and squirming in its own blood. Even the most tenderhearted person would not have been moved to save such a grotesque creature in such a miserable state.

Nevertheless, God, being rich in mercy, because of His great love with which He loved us, even when we were dead in our transgressions, made us alive together with Christ.[3]

The glory of the gospel is not that God saves worthy creatures whose beauty draws out His love and makes it impossible for Him to live without us. The glory of the gospel is that God saves vile and wretched sinners who have utterly defiled themselves, evoking disdain and abandonment from all except a God who *is* love.

THE GLORY OF GOD

We have made a brief departure from Ezekiel 36:22–28 to consider the unmerited love of God as a primary motivation for His saving work among undeserving sinners. Now we will return to the text to find the great motivation behind all of God's works: the promotion of His own glory. In summary, God saves people for His own sake and according to His own good pleasure. The language of these verses may seem strange, even offensive, not only to the secular mind but also to a contemporary Christianity that is drenched in humanism.

The first outstanding truth brought to our attention is that God is not motivated to save Israel because of any virtue in Israel. Twice in this brief text, God points out that Israel had done nothing but profane or violate the honor of His name among the nations. The apostle Paul goes so far as to say that the name of God was blasphemed among the Gentiles because of Israel's idolatrous practices and evil deeds.[4] God did not find in Israel a reason for saving but rather for condemning.

If such things can be said about the nation of Israel, how much more do they apply to the pagan nations around the globe? If the Jews, who had the law and the testimonies of God, were utterly void of virtue and merit, how much more is the darkened and hardened pagan? The failure of the Jews eliminates their boasting as well as that of the entire world.[5] Thus, we must all stand with our hands over our mouths as our verdict is read:

---

3. Ephesians 2:4–5
4. Romans 2:24
5. Romans 3:19

There is none righteous, no, not one;
There is none who understands;
There is none who seeks after God.
They have all turned aside;
They have together become unprofitable;
There is none who does good, no, not one (Rom. 3:10–12).

If God finds no reason in us to save us, then why does He do so? We find the answer in the text: "I do not do this for your sake...but for My holy name's sake," and again, "I will sanctify My great name...and the nations shall know that I am the LORD." God has determined to save a people for Himself from the midst of the nations, and He has determined to do so for His own glory, for the sake of His own great name, and for the sake of His praise, that all might know that He alone is God. As God declares through the prophet Jeremiah:

I will cleanse them from all their iniquity by which they have sinned against Me, and I will pardon all their iniquities by which they have sinned and by which they have transgressed against Me. Then it shall be to Me a name of joy, a praise, and an honor before all nations of the earth, who shall hear all the good that I do to them; they shall fear and tremble for all the goodness and all the prosperity that I provide for it (Jer. 33:8–9).

Here God clearly communicates to us His motive for the salvation of His people: for all the goodness He shows them, He will gain for Himself praise, glory, and reverence from all who hear of it.

It is important to note that God's passion for His own glory is a theme that runs throughout the full course of divine revelation. The Scriptures teach that the creation of the universe, the fall of man, the nation of Israel, the cross of Christ, the church, and the judgment of the nations have one great and final purpose: the glory of God. In other words, God does all that He does in order that He might reveal the fullness of all that He is to His creation, and that He might be esteemed, worshiped, and enjoyed as God. Some of church history's most eminent theologians heartily accept this interpretation of the text. Charles Hodge writes, "Men have long endeavored to find a satisfactory answer to the question, Why God created the world? What end was it designed to accomplish?... The only satisfactory method of determining the question is by appealing to the Scriptures. There it is explicitly taught that the glory of God, the manifestation of His perfections, is the last end of all His works."[6] Jonathan Edwards writes, "Thus we see that the great end of God's works, which is so variously expressed in Scripture, is indeed but ONE; and this one end is most properly and comprehensively called, THE GLORY OF GOD."[7]

God's passion for His own glory is the clear and unapologetic teaching of Scripture, yet many people, sometimes even sincere Christians, ask whether it is right for God to act for His own glory. To answer this question, we need to consider only who God is. According to the Scriptures, He is *infinitely greater* than all His creation combined. Therefore, it is not only right but also necessary for Him to take the highest place and make His glory the great reason or chief end of all that He does. It is right for Him to take center stage and work all things so that His glory (i.e., the fullness of who He is) might be made known to all, to the end that He might be glorified (i.e., esteemed and worshiped) above all. For Him to shun such preeminence would be for Him to deny that He is God. For anyone other than God to seek such preeminence would be the grossest form of idolatry. Again, this is the common consensus of theologian and preacher alike. A. A. Hodge writes, "Since God Himself is infinitely worthier than the sum of all creatures, it follows that the manifestation of His own excellence is...the highest and worthiest end conceivable."[8] Charles Spurgeon writes, "God must have the highest motive, and there can be no higher motive conceivable than His own glory."[9]

A second truth we must understand is that God does not seek His own glory apart from His creatures' greatest good. In fact, the greatest good God could ever accomplish for His creatures and the greatest kindness He could ever show them is to glorify Himself—to direct and work in all things so that He might display the fullness of all that He is before them. If God is of infinite value, splendor, and beauty, then it follows that the most valuable, most splendid, and most beautiful gift He could ever give to His creatures is the revelation of Himself. With regard to this precious truth, Louis Berkhof writes: "In seeking self-expression for

6. Charles Hodge, *Systematic Theology*, ed. Edward N. Gross (Grand Rapids: Baker, 1988), 1:565, 567.

7. Jonathan Edwards, *Dissertation on the End for Which God Created the* World, in *The Works of Jonathan Edwards* (Edinburgh: Banner of Truth, 1974), 1:119.

8. A. A. Hodge, *Outlines of Theology* (Edinburgh: Banner of Truth, 1972), 245.

9. C. H. Spurgeon, *The Metropolitan Tabernacle Pulpit: Containing Sermons Preached and Revised* (Pasadena, Tex.: Pilgrim Publications, 1969–1980), 10:304.

the glory of His name, God did not disregard the well-being, the highest good of others, but promoted it…. The supreme end of God in creation, the manifestation of His glory, therefore, includes, as subordinate ends, the happiness and salvation of His creatures, and the reception of praise from grateful and adoring hearts."[10]

We have learned that God glorifies Himself by directing and working in all things so that He might reveal the fullness of all that He is to His creation. This is especially true with regard to the cross of Christ and the salvation that He accomplished through it. In this one thing, the fullness of God's attributes is revealed in the greatest possible way in order that God might be esteemed, worshiped, and enjoyed to the greatest possible degree by both the angels and the redeemed. Why has God given His Son for the salvation of wicked people? Do not look for the reason in a fallen humanity that is ruined of worth and destitute of merit. Look to God! He has accomplished this great work of salvation for the sake of His name and the praise of His own glory! If this bothers us, then we should understand that if God had not acted for His own sake, He would have had no reason to act for ours.

This truth should not only inspire awe, but it also has great practical implications, especially with regard to our salvation. It is for this reason God never fails in the work of salvation that He has begun in the life of the believer. He who began a good work in us will always perfect it because His reputation is on the line.[11] Salvation is a work of God and arguably His greatest achievement. Failure in this singular endeavor would bring blight to His glory. This truth is wonderfully illustrated in Moses' account of Israel's rebellion and his intercession on their behalf.

After the spies' report and Israel's refusal to enter the Promised Land, God threatened their total annihilation. In the face of divine judgment, Moses interceded with the following argument:

> Now if You kill these people as one man, then the nations which have heard of Your fame will speak, saying, "Because the Lord was not able to bring this people to the land which He swore to give them, therefore He killed them in the wilderness." And now, I pray, let the power of my Lord be great…. Pardon the iniquity of this people, I pray, according to the greatness of Your mercy (Num. 14:15–19).

---

10. Louis Berkhof, *Systematic Theology* (repr., Edinburgh: Banner of Truth, 1998), 136–37.
11. Philippians 1:6

Moses' argument grows out of his passion for the glory of God, and his logic is superb: If God utterly rejected His people and failed to bring them into the Promised Land, the nations would attribute the failure to God's inability. In the same way, God will not abandon His work of salvation in the individual believer, but He who began the good work will carry it on to completion until that final day.[12] God's perseverance and unfailing commitment to His people's salvation has His glory as its end.

And the nations shall know that I am the Lord (Ezek. 36:23).

Then it shall be to Me a name of joy, a praise, and an honor before all nations of the earth, who shall hear all the good that I do to them; they shall fear and tremble for all the goodness and all the prosperity that I provide for it (Jer. 33:9).

For from the rising of the sun, even to its going down, My name shall be great among the Gentiles (Mal. 1:11).

---

12. Philippians 1:6

CHAPTER SEVEN

The Author of Salvation

For I will take you from among the nations, gather you out of all countries, and bring you into your own land. Then I will sprinkle clean water on you, and you shall be clean; I will cleanse you from all your filthiness and from all your idols. I will give you a new heart and put a new spirit within you; I will take the heart of stone out of your flesh and give you a heart of flesh. I will put My Spirit within you and cause you to walk in My statutes, and you will keep My judgments and do them. Then you shall dwell in the land that I gave to your fathers; you shall be My people, and I will be your God.

—Ezekiel 36:24–28

Since we have considered the divine motive for God's seeking the salvation of wicked people, we will now consider the actual work of conversion in the individual believer. Ezekiel 36:24–28 is one of the most beautiful and powerful Old Testament prophecies concerning the new covenant that was to be inaugurated by the coming of the Messiah and His work of redemption. It provides us with one of the clearest illustrations of the doctrines of regeneration and conversion found anywhere in the Scriptures.

For the believer who understands the content of this text, it has a twofold purpose. First, it provides a standard by which we can measure the validity of our profession of faith in Christ and obtain a biblical assurance. This text teaches us that genuine conversion is the result of a supernatural work of God, by which the very heart or nature of a person is changed, making him responsive to the will of God. Thus, God's ongoing work of sanctification and a growing submission to His will marks the life of the truly converted. Second, this text is an inexhaustible source of joy, consolation, and comfort. In the believer's pilgrimage, the progress is often slow and thwarted by many setbacks and deviations. He wonders if he will ever advance or overcome the sins that beset him and hinder his running.[1] This text assures every believer that He who began a good work will perfect it, that He will cleanse us from all our filthiness and idols, and that He will cause us to walk in His statutes.[2]

The first great truth that we will consider from this text is that God is both the author and finisher of our salvation, that the salvation of a person individually, and that of the church collectively, is the work of God. He initiates it, sees to its perseverance, and brings it to its ultimate consummation on the day of Christ Jesus. More than a cliché, the sovereignty of God is here brilliantly displayed as the foundation of the believer's hope and the source of his strength. The certainty with which God speaks is unmistakable. This is apparent in the following phrases from the text. We should notice the use of the first person pronoun "I" (God is the one who acts), followed by an unconditional promise (He will not fail):

"I will take you from the nations."

"[I will] gather you from all the lands."

"[I will] bring you into your own land."

"I will sprinkle clean water on you."

"I will cleanse you from all your filthiness and from all your idols."

"I will give you a new heart and put a new spirit within you."

"I will take the heart of stone from out of your flesh and give you a heart of flesh."

"I will put My Spirit within you."

"[I will] cause you to walk in My statutes."

There is not the least measure of doubt or uncertainty in these affirmations. God is not musing aloud or granting us audience to His hopes and dreams. He is not speaking about what He would do if He could gain our cooperation. Rather, He speaks as one who "does whatever He pleases" and who "works all things according to the counsel of His will" (Ps. 115:3; Eph. 1:11). Notice also that God is not only telling us what He will do in the life of every Christian, but He is also guaranteeing the outcome of His work:

---

1. Hebrews 12:1
2. Philippians 1:6

"You shall be clean."

You will "walk in My statutes, and you will keep My judgments and do them."

You will "dwell in the land that I gave to your fathers."

"You shall be My people, and I will be your God."

Behold the power of God in the salvation of His church and in the conversion of each of its members! Without fail, those whom He calls, He also recreates; and those whom He recreates, He also cleanses; and those whom He cleanses, He also indwells; and those whom He indwells, He also causes to walk in His statutes and makes them careful to observe His ordinances. Here we have a golden chain of salvation like the one the apostle Paul penned in his letter to the church in Rome.[3] Like Paul, we can exclaim, "What then shall we say to these things? If God is for us, who can be against us?" (Rom. 8:31).

He who began a good work in us will perfect it by His own doing. This is not a denial of human responsibility in salvation or of the Christian's great struggle against sin. This does not negate that there will be great losses as well as victories in our striving for conformity to Christ. However, it does assure us that God has set out to make for Himself a people, and by His own power, He will see it done. All whom He calls will come to Him, and of those who come to Him, not one will be lost.[4] Through the blood of Christ, they are justified, and through the power of the Holy Spirit, they are regenerated, sanctified, and led.[5] Although each may grow at a different pace and to a different degree and some may seem to fly to maturity while others barely crawl, they will all, nevertheless, progress toward the upward call of God in Christ and demonstrate in word and deed that they are His people and He has become their God.[6]

---

3. Romans 8:29–30 is often referred to as the "Golden Chain of Salvation," in that it sets forth with absolute certainty each aspect of the saving work of God in the life of the believer—election, predestination, justification, sanctification (assumed), and glorification: "For whom He foreknew, He also predestined to be conformed to the image of His Son, that He might be the firstborn among many brethren. Moreover whom He predestined, these He also called; whom He called, these He also justified; and whom He justified, these He also glorified."

4. John 6:37, 39; 18:9

5. John 3:3–8; Romans 5:9; 6:11; 8:14; 1 Corinthians 6:11; Galatians 5:18; Titus 3:5

6. Philippians 3:14

The reader must grasp these essential truths of conversion as this text reveals them. Repeatedly it must be proclaimed that genuine biblical conversion will yield its fruit in the life of every believer—although the fruit may vary, and some will bring forth a hundredfold, while others bring forth sixty, and still others only thirty.[7] Nevertheless, they will all bring forth fruit, and by their fruit they will be known.[8] This certainty is not primarily a result of their commitment, but a result of the nature of conversion. Those who are justified by faith alone have become God's "workmanship, created in Christ Jesus for good works, which God prepared beforehand that [they] should walk in them" (Eph. 2:10).

---

7. Matthew 13:23
8. Matthew 7:16–20

CHAPTER EIGHT

Separation and Cleansing

For I will take you from among the nations, gather you out of all coun-
tries, and bring you into your own land. Then I will sprinkle clean water
on you, and you shall be clean; I will cleanse you from all your filthiness
and from all your idols.
                                                        —Ezekiel 36:24–25

In this day, when the growth of Christianity in the West seems to be
directly related to the growth of carnality in the church, it is important
to ask what the true nature or essential characteristics of biblical conversion are. What happens, and what does it look like when a person is born
again? We can be thankful that for us, and the church at large, these
questions are answered in a powerful and illustrative manner in the new
covenant promise recorded in Ezekiel 36:22–28.

In the following chapters, we will consider some of these essential
characteristics of true conversion, not necessarily in chronological order
as they appear in conversion, but as the text gives them to us. Throughout our study, we would do well to ask ourselves to what degree these
marks of conversion are discernible realities in our lives. In the words of
the apostle Paul, we should test and examine ourselves to see if we are
in the faith.[1]

THE DIVINE WORK OF SEPARATION
One of the first noticeable results of true conversion is biblical separation from the world—a gradual divorce or withdrawing from all that is
displeasing to God and in opposition to His will. Such a separation is not
an end in itself, but rather the first and essential step to a greater end: a

---

1. 2 Corinthians 13:5

drawing nigh unto God, and the giving of ourselves to His purposes and will. This truth is both promised and beautifully illustrated in Ezekiel 36:24. Through the prophet Ezekiel, God declares to His people, "For I will take you from among the nations, gather you out of all countries, and bring you into your own land."

This new covenant promise does not find its ultimate fulfillment in the mere physical return of the nation of Israel from her captivity in Babylon, but rather it looks forward to the day when God would call forth His people, Jew and Gentile alike, from all nations and gather them together under the banner of His dear Son. Furthermore, through the work of regeneration and sanctification, God promises not only to take His people out of the pagan nations, but also to take the influence of the pagan nations out of His people. He would draw them to Himself. He would be their God, and they would be His people.

As we approach this text, one of the first truths that comes to our attention is that God is the cause or prime mover in separating His people from the worldliness that surrounds them. Although biblical separation involves human responsibility, it is primarily a work of God, which He also guarantees. God *will* draw His people away from the moral corruption of this fallen world, and He *will* bring them unto Himself. The Christian *will* gradually grow apart from the ideals and pleasures of this present age, and he *will* learn to walk with God and cling to His commands. Our text and many others throughout the Scriptures guarantee such progress. God is the author and finisher of our faith.[2] We are God's workmanship.[3] He who began a good work in us will complete it.[4]

Over the last several decades of Western Christianity, it seems that many great and precious truths have been discarded—or at least forgotten. One such truth is that the church and the individual believer are God's possession. He lays absolute claim upon them by virtue of creation and redemption. He has both made them and bought them with a price.[5] Therefore, they are His to do with them as He wills. Under the old covenant, God told Israel, "You shall be My own possession among all the peoples, for all the earth is Mine."[6] In the new covenant, God says the

---

2. Hebrews 12:2
3. Ephesians 2:10
4. Philippians 1:6
5. 1 Corinthians 6:20; 7:23; Colossians 1:16
6. Exodus 19:5

same to the church. We are God's possession to the praise of His glory and to proclaim His excellencies throughout the universe.[7] For this reason, Christ died in order to redeem us from every lawless deed and to purify for Himself a people for His own possession, zealous for good deeds.[8]

Doesn't God have the right to do as He pleases with His own? If we belong to Him by the twofold claim of creation and redemption, doesn't He have the right to separate us from the herd of humanity and claim us for Himself, for His good pleasure, and for His eternal purposes? The Scriptures answer all these questions with a resounding and unapologetic yes.

Another equally forsaken truth is that God is a jealous God who will not share His people's affection with another.[9] This is why He commanded Israel not to worship or serve any other gods.[10] For the same reason, He warns the church and the individual believer that friendship with the world is hostility toward Him, for He jealously desires the Spirit that He has made to dwell in us.[11] Although this doctrine of divine jealousy has been greatly maligned, it is one of the most beautiful truths in Scripture. It is the proof of God's unchanging love for His people. We would doubt the love of any husband who was willing to share his spouse with every other man. Should we think less of God's love? Furthermore, the most loving thing God can do for His people is keep them from other loves that cannot truly satisfy and will only lead to their great harm.

Founded upon these two truths of a right to ownership and a jealous love, God works in the life of all believers to separate them from the false loves and moral corruption of this fallen world and draws us to Himself as a treasured and transformed possession. To achieve this desired end, He will spare no expense, employ every means, and exhaust every resource. As God declared through the prophet Jeremiah, He will bring His people to the end He has chosen for them, and He will do so, "with all [His] heart and with all [His] soul" (Jer. 32:41). In other words, He will employ the fullness of His deity to assure the completion of the work.

Before we continue, we must ask a question: Is God's work of separation a reality in our lives? From the moment of our conversion until the present, can we trace a history of God's providentially working in our

---

7. Ephesians 1:14; 1 Peter 2:9
8. Titus 2:14
9. Exodus 34:14
10. Exodus 20:4–5
11. James 4:5

lives to draw us away from the moral corruption of this world and to Himself? This is the testimony and legacy of every true Christian. If such a work of sanctification is wanting or indiscernible in our lives, it is a call to examine ourselves, even test ourselves, to see if we are in the faith.[12]

THE DIVINE WORK OF CLEANSING

One characteristic that all fallen people share is their moral uncleanness. The psalmist declared that we have all turned aside and together have become corrupt, to such a degree that there is no one who does good, not even one.[13] The prophet Isaiah cried out that we have all become like one who is unclean, and all our righteous deeds are like a filthy garment.[14] The patriarch Job discerned man's moral filth to be so pervasive that he rightly determined it to be beyond all human remedy.[15]

The testimony of Scripture against humanity is not flattering, but it is true. Every page of human history bears witness to the fact that fallen man is radically depraved, morally corrupt, and beyond the aid of any human remedy. This is why God's promise that He will make us clean from all our filthiness and idols in Ezekiel 36:24–25 ought to be a cause for great joy.

The Christian religion is unique from all others in that it requires cleansing but negates the possibility that human endeavor can achieve it. Unlike other religions, it utterly denounces all human attempts at self-liberation from moral bondage or self-cleansing from moral filth. In turn, it offers helpless people a God who alone can both liberate and cleanse. As He declared through the prophet Isaiah, "I, even I, am the LORD, and besides Me there is no savior" (Isa. 43:11).

In Ezekiel 36:24–25, God promises a divine work of cleansing for all those whom He separates unto Himself. From the Scriptures, we understand that this cleansing is both positional and experimental. It has to do with both justification and sanctification. The two are twin graces and, therefore, inseparable. Those whom God justifies, He also sanctifies.

According to the Scriptures, a person is justified, or declared right with God, the moment he turns from self-reliance and places his faith in

---

12. 2 Corinthians 13:5
13. Psalm 14:3
14. Isaiah 64:6
15. Job 9:29–31

the atoning work of Christ. At that moment, his position before God is as the psalmist declares: his transgressions have been forgiven, his sins have been covered, and they are no longer taken into account.[16] To use another metaphor, it is as though his sins have been cleansed with hyssop, and he has been washed to be whiter than snow.[17] Even the penetrating eye of a holy and omniscient God can find no spot or blemish in him.[18]

The doctrine of justification by faith is one of the most majestic and comforting doctrines in the Scriptures, but it never appears alone in the life of the Christian. The work of progressive sanctification, a grace of equal beauty, always accompanies it. Through justification, the believer is once for all declared clean before the throne of God from guilt and condemnation of every moral filth and idolatry. In addition, the righteousness of Christ is imputed to him so that he becomes the very righteousness of God.[19] However, through the continuing and progressive work of sanctification, the justified believer is gradually transformed into the likeness of Christ. By means of divine providence and the ministry of the Spirit and the Word, God progressively cleanses the believer of the filth that clings to him and destroys the idols in his life that challenge God's supremacy and compete for his loyalty. God's work of justification in our lives is a finished work: there is nothing left to be completed and nothing that can be added to it. However, God's work of sanctification in our lives is an ongoing and progressive work that will not be completed until we stand before Him in glory. Again, justification and sanctification are always found together. Justification makes sanctification possible, and sanctification is the evidence that we have been justified.

Like every other promise in Ezekiel 36:23–28, God's work of sanctification in the life of the believer is not mere wishful thinking based on some unfounded hope, but it is an absolute certainty, based upon an immutable divine decree. Although many battles mark the Christian life, and although the Christian will experience losses as well as victories, the God who began a good work in him will complete it.[20] The sins that beset him *will* gradually be removed, and the idols that beckon him away from God *will* be destroyed. Although the believer will never be

---

16. Psalm 32:1–2; Romans 4:7–8
17. Psalm 51:7
18. Song of Solomon 4:7
19. 2 Corinthians 5:21
20. Philippians 1:6

without sin in this life, he will make progress in the things of God and grow in conformity to the person of Jesus Christ. God will assert His sovereignty and direct all things in the life of the believer to this end, and He will do so for the glory of His name and the good of His people. He will see to its accomplishment. This truth is illustrated in the following account.

Imagine a farm boy raised in the American Midwest. Every day, from dawn to dusk, he works and plays in the cow barns and plowed furrows of the field. Every evening he returns to the house encased in dirt. Before he can make his way through the door of the house, his mother always meets him on the porch with a simple directive: "Drop your clothes in the laundry, and go directly to the bath!"

Although he is normally compliant, one evening the boy foolishly decides to exercise autonomy and informs his mother that he will not be bathing. He says he is too tired and simply isn't very dirty. His mother quickly resolves the conflict by exercising her rightful authority as a parent. She walks into his room, looks him in the eye, and declares, "Young man, you *will* take a bath!"

Knowing he has no choice against true parental authority, he grudgingly makes his way to the bathroom, turns on the faucet, and dabs a few drops of water on the areas with the most obvious concentrations of dirt. He quickly dries with a towel and covers the dirt that remains with his pajamas. Everything is going as planned until his mother walks into the bathroom. She spies the deplorable condition of her previously clean white towels and the less than pristine condition of the bath tiles under the boy's feet. She lifts his chin, revealing the dirt still encased around his neck. She rolls back his pajama sleeves and pant legs, exposing the dirt that remains on his elbows and knees. In response, she again exercises her parental authority and commands that he strip down and return to the bathtub. To the boy's horror, she then proceeds to draw new water and lather the soap. She says, "You are my child, and you *will* be clean!"

The boy's mother had lived most of her adult life on the farm. Though she was truly a lady, she could outwork most men—and often did. She wrangled cattle, hauled hay, and had hands as calloused as any laborer. When she finished bathing any of her children, they were clean. It felt as though she had not only taken off the dirt but that she had also removed at least one layer of skin. When this mother bathed her children, they came forth clean!

Note that during those times when the boy's mother intervened in the bathing of her child, no one discussed the question of sovereignty and free will. No one would have indicted the mother for abusing her authority or violating the free will of her child. She was simply exercising her parental right over her child, who was often apathetic and careless, and sometimes even reluctant and disobedient.

The question before us is this: Has Western evangelicalism concluded that God has no right to exercise His authority over anyone, even His own children? Should an earthly mother be granted more authority over her children than God is allowed over His? Someone has rightly stated that the God of American Christianity is the only omnipotent and supreme Lord of all who has no authority to do anything unless He is first granted permission. He can save His children from hell, but He has no right to demand anything from them lest He violate some twisted notion of human autonomy.

Imagine the absurdity, even obscenity, of the following scenario: The courts examine the father of several small children because of their malnourished state and unkempt appearance. In defense, he assures the court that every day he prepares the children's meals, makes sure they take their bath, and lays out fresh clothing. Nevertheless, in spite of his diligence, the children simply refuse to comply. Although he truly desires the best for his children, his unalterable regard for their freedom makes it impossible for him to intervene. The courts will not applaud the father for his respect for human autonomy, but rather they will censure him for his irrational behavior leading to neglect.

The growing number of alcohol-related driving accidents and deaths have increased at an alarming rate, and in response, one media campaign employs the slogan "friends don't let friends drive drunk." The idea is that a true friend will do everything in his power to keep a friend from getting behind the wheel of a car while he is under the influence of alcohol. It is striking that no one argues against such an intervention in defense of human autonomy. In fact, no one considers the matter. To let a friend drive while he is intoxicated in order to honor his free will is not considered virtuous, but rather immoral or even criminal.

The present popular views regarding the work of God and human autonomy are not only contrary to sound judgment, but they are also foreign to the Scriptures. First, the God of the Bible is the Lord who "works all things according to the counsel of His will" (Eph. 1:11). Surely the one who "brings the counsel of the nations to nothing" and "makes the plans of the peoples of no effect" reserves for Himself the right to govern His own people according to His purposes and for their good (Ps. 33:10). For this reason the writer of Proverbs unapologetically declared, "A man's heart plans his way, but the LORD directs his steps," and, "There are many plans in a man's heart, nevertheless the Lord's counsel—that will stand" (16:9; 19:21). We should not be alarmed and run to the defense of our supposed autonomy because God has a plan for the life of every believer and will exercise His power to accomplish it. Instead, this truth should be a great cause for comfort and hope, as the prophet Jeremiah explains: "For I know the thoughts that I think toward you, says the LORD, thoughts of peace and not of evil, to give you a future and a hope" (Jer. 29:11).

As their creator and redeemer, God has the divine right to work in the lives of His people according to His good pleasure. The prophet Isaiah tells us that to oppose this right or to argue to the contrary is tantamount to rebellion, quarreling with our maker.[21] It is to turn things around, to reverse the created order, and to consider the clay equal to the potter.[22] Rather than tenaciously defending our supposed rights as creatures, we ought to concentrate on honoring God's right as creator and redeemer. We would do well to adopt Isaiah's attitude of submission before God's gracious providence, and cry out:

> But now, O LORD,
> You are our Father;
> We are the clay, and You our potter;
> And all we are the work of Your hand (Isa. 64:8).

Christians who have walked at length with God would describe the Christian life as a demonstration of God's enduring faithfulness, not only to save them from the condemnation of sin but also to sanctify them. As the Christian looks back on his life, he sees countless demonstrations of God's providence effectually working to cleanse him from all his filthiness and idolatries.

Is this cleansing and idolatry-destroying of God a reality in our lives? As we look back across the years of our pilgrimage, can we see God burning the dross off us like a refiner's fire and purifying us like a launderer's

---

21. Isaiah 45:9
22. Isaiah 29:16

soap?[23] Can we see Him tearing down the idols in our lives as He tore down Dagon and smashed him to pieces in his own temple?[24] If we are truly Christian, God's claim upon us and His work of sanctification in our lives will be evident, not only to us, but also to those around us. Over the many years of our Christian life, we will experience progress in the things of Christ and greater conformity to His image. For we are His workmanship, and He who began a good work in us will finish it.[25] As He has promised, "I will sprinkle clean water on you and you will be clean. I will cleanse you from all your filthiness and idols."

THE DIVINE WORK OF DISCIPLINE

We cannot conclude a study of the divine works of separation and cleansing without a consideration of one of the primary means that God employs to achieve these wonderful goals: divine discipline. The believer's God is both loving and wise. He weighs eternity as having an infinitely greater significance than all temporal pleasures combined. He clearly sees that the greatest good for His children is their conformity to the image of Christ.[26] Thus, He will employ whatever righteous means necessary to transform His people: teaching, reproof, correction, and training.[27] Sometimes such discipline is light, and at other times, it is severe; yet God always administers it with love and the greatest good of the believer in mind. He loves us too much to allow us to remain as we are. His providence will even expose us to the greatest of temporal sufferings, if through them we might gain an extra weight of glory beyond all comparison.[28]

An extraordinary example of such divine discipline occurred in the life of the patriarch Jacob. In the word of the Lord through Malachi to a wayward Israel, God made the following declaration: "Yet Jacob I have loved; but Esau I have hated" (Mal. 1:2–3). In context, the nation of Israel was suffering from political and economic destitution. God had delivered them from captivity and brought them back into their land. However, it

---

23. Malachi 3:2
24. 1 Samuel 5:2–7
25. Ephesians 2:10; Philippians 1:6
26. Romans 8:28–29
27. 2 Timothy 3:16
28. 2 Corinthians 4:17

seemed that divine discipline had not ended and that the promised prosperity was nowhere in sight. For this reason, Israel had become weary and
prone to doubt God's covenant love. To remedy their doubt, the prophet
Malachi directed them to contrast God's dealings with Jacob (Israel) with
those of his brother, Esau (Edom). Yes, Israel had suffered great discipline
from the hand of God, but it was for their redemption. Though Edom
remained unscathed and even seemed to prosper from Israel's loss, it
was a sign of God's rejection of them and their ultimate destruction. In
other words, the prophet Malachi was reminding a doubting Israel that
correction and discipline were demonstrations of God's covenant love
rather than a cause for denying it. The wisdom of Proverbs strongly sup-
ports His logic:

> My son, do not despise the chastening of the LORD,
> Nor detest His correction;
> For whom the LORD loves He corrects,
> Just as a father the son in whom he delights (3:11–12).

We see how the truth of this text applies to the Christian when we
examine the individual lives of Jacob and Esau and God's dealings with
them. How is it that God demonstrated His love toward Jacob while demonstrating His hatred or wrath toward Esau? In the case of Jacob, it was by
separating him, taking ownership of his life, and working to conform him
to His will. In the case of Esau, it was by cutting him loose, leaving him
to himself, and giving him free rein to be as the rest of the pagan world.

When we examine Esau's life, we discover that God fulfilled every
promise He ever made to Isaac concerning him. He had broken free from
the yoke of his brother Jacob and had become so prosperous that he had
no need of Jacob's support or blessing.[29] However, we see God's rejection
of and wrath toward Esau in His not intervening in Esau's life. There is
no work of separation and sanctification. He leaves Esau to himself to
become the epitome of the godless man.[30]

In contrast, when we examine Jacob's life, we discover God working
in every step, teaching, guiding, and disciplining with amazing thoroughness and even severity. In fact, the discipline was so heavy upon
Jacob's life that when he returned to the Promised Land, he was limping.[31]

---

29. Genesis 27:40; 33:9
30. Hebrews 12:16
31. Genesis 32:31

Divine providence had taken its toll on Jacob's body, but it had transformed him from a deceiver into a broken, but obedient son. In this way, God deals with all His legitimate children: "For whom the LORD loves He chastens, and scourges every son whom He receives" (Heb. 12:6).

We learn from this text that one of the greatest evidences of true conversion is divine discipline leading to holiness. In love, God has committed Himself to every one of His children. He will encourage, instruct, and discipline them for their own good so that they may share His holiness.[32] He will take them from the nations, gather them from all the lands, and bring them into the land and life He has prepared for them.

Often Christians regard as a burden the very thing they ought to esteem a blessing. At times, a believer will complain that others around him are free to break God's law without the slightest consequence, while they are disciplined for the slightest infraction. This should not be a cause for complaint, but for rejoicing and praise. It is great evidence of the new birth. It is proof of sonship: "If you endure chastening, God deals with you as with sons; for what son is there whom a father does not chasten? But if you are without chastening, of which all have become partakers, then you are illegitimate and not sons" (Heb. 12:7–8).

Imagine a young boy sent to school on the first day after summer vacation. His mother dresses him in his new school clothes and warns him to come straight home at the end of class. He is not to stay behind with his friends or stop by the local creek to play. However, on the way home, temptation overcomes reason, and he follows his friends to the creek. Before he knows it, a minute has turned into an hour, and his clean clothes have turned into filthy rags. Realizing his error and the consequences that await him, he returns home with two of his equally disobedient friends at his side. When his mother sees him and pronounces discipline, he quickly points to the other boys and questions the justice of punishing him while letting the others go free. His mother's reply is brief, but effective: "They are not my children, and they are not under my care. However, you are my child, and to you alone will my discipline be directed."

The moral of the story is this: Discipline is the evidence of a parent/child relationship and not the negation of it. The mother's relationship to the child and her love and concern for the child's well-being are what

---

32. Hebrews 12:10

moved her to administer both correction and discipline. Again, the writer of Hebrews brings out this point clearly: "Furthermore, we have had human fathers who corrected us, and we paid them respect. Shall we not much more readily be in subjection to the Father of spirits and live? For they indeed for a few days chastened us as seemed best to them, but He for our profit, that we may be partakers of His holiness" (12:9–10).

There is a sense in which God takes possession of each of His children. He hems them in and leads them in a way that promotes His purpose of holiness in their lives. Although it is not always evident, He is constantly working, teaching, correcting, punishing, and disciplining. His love for His people makes Him a relentless worker in their lives. He will not lay down His hammer and chisel until His work is done.

God is not as some would suppose Him to be: a derelict and disinterested father. He will not allow His children to run the streets of this world unattended. He is not a hired shepherd who is unconcerned about the wanderings of His flock. However, those who believe that a Christian can walk in a continuous and unaltered state of carnality all the days of his life are making just such an accusation! Rather than exalting the grace of God, they are turning it into a license for sin.[33] Rather than exalting the forbearance of God, they are portraying Him as an uninvolved or impotent father. Rather than exalting the gospel, they are declaring it void of power. This great error results in the unbelieving world's blasphemy. As the apostle Paul wrote, "The name of God is blasphemed among the Gentiles because of you" (Rom. 2:24).

As we close this chapter, a few questions remain for each of us who confesses the name of Jesus: Is there evidence of divine providence working in our lives to both separate us from the world and draw us unto God? When we look back on our lives since our conversion, do we find proof of God's separating and sanctifying work? Are we becoming that peculiar people who belong to Him alone? When we walk with Him, do we feel His pleasure? When we turn away, do we know His correction? Does His loving parental discipline mark our lives? We must ask these questions. The reality of God's sanctifying work in our lives should bring us great assurance. The lack of such should bring us great concern.

---

33. Jude 4

CHAPTER NINE

A New Heart

I will give you a new heart and put a new spirit within you; I will take the heart of stone out of your flesh and give you a heart of flesh.
—Ezekiel 36:26

In Ezekiel 36:26, we find one of Scripture's most picturesque and instructive descriptions of the doctrine of regeneration. It is essential that we not only come to a biblical understanding of this doctrine but that we also comprehend something of its vast importance. It is not an exaggeration to say that our understanding of regeneration will determine both our view of conversion and our methodology in evangelism.

The doctrine of regeneration refers to the supernatural work of the Spirit of God whereby the spiritually dead sinner is made alive, his radically depraved nature is transformed, and he is enabled to respond to the gospel call with repentance and faith in Jesus Christ. The Westminster Confession and 1689 London Baptist Confession describe the Spirit's work of regeneration as "enlightening the mind spiritually and savingly to understand the things of God, taking away the heart of stone, and replacing it with an heart of flesh; renewing the will,...and effectually drawing [persons] to Jesus Christ: yet so, as they come most freely, being made willing by His grace."[1]

The word *regeneration* comes from a Latin verb that means to create again.[2] The New Testament writers use a variety of phrases and terminology to describe the doctrine. In the gospel of John, Jesus describes regeneration as being born anew, or being born from above.[3] In his first

---

1. Westminster Confession of Faith, chapter 10; 1689 London Baptist Confession, chapter 10.
2. Latin: *regenerare*.
3. John 3:3, 6–7; Greek: *gennáo ánothen*.

epistle, the apostle Peter uses a singular Greek verb that means to be born again or born anew.[4] The apostle Paul describes the doctrine of regeneration as being made alive and being raised from the dead to walk in newness of life.[5] It is such a radical and comprehensive work of the Spirit that he considers anyone in Christ to be a new creation or creature.[6]

In this text from Ezekiel we see all these truths powerfully and beautifully illustrated. According to the ancient prophet, the doctrine of regeneration goes far beyond a mere surface reformation or change in behavior due to some discipline of the will. It involves an ontological change.[7] The very nature of the person is undone and recreated. The heart of stone that cannot respond to divine stimuli is transformed into a heart of flesh that will respond.

To illustrate, let us say that we are standing before a stone statue made in the perfect likeness of a man. It bears exact resemblance to an intellectual and volitional creature. Nevertheless, it is made of stone, and therefore is inanimate. We may kick it, prod it, and even set it on fire, but it will not respond. It is a lifeless stone and therefore unable to react to any sort of stimuli. However, if we had the power to change the stone into living flesh, the result of all our prodding and poking would be quite different. Healthy, living flesh possesses a high degree of sensitivity and the ability not only to feel but also to react. Healthy flesh discerns the lightest breeze on the skin and notices even the slightest touch of a finger. It possesses the power to respond in direct accord with the stimuli given it.

In a similar fashion, the sinner is spiritually dead and unable to respond to divine stimuli. This lack of ability does not excuse him from guilt or make him any less responsible to God, because his inability is his own doing. The sinner cannot respond positively to God because he will not. Although he possesses the necessary capacity to both know God and understand His revealed will, he suppresses what he knows to be true.[8] His love for unrighteousness and desire for autonomy makes him so hostile to God that he simply cannot bring himself to acknowledge Him or obey His law.

---

4. 1 Peter 1:3, 23; Greek: *anagennáo*.
5. Romans 6:4; Ephesians 2:4–5
6. 2 Corinthians 5:17
7. That which relates to the very being, nature, or existence of a person or thing.
8. Romans 1:18–32

This hard truth about man is best illustrated in the relationship between the patriarch Joseph and his brothers. The Scriptures declare that Joseph's brothers "could not" speak to him on friendly terms, because "they hated him" (Gen. 37:4). Here we clearly see illustrated the doctrine of moral inability. Joseph's brothers possessed the necessary capacity to communicate with him and even speak kind words to him. However, they were unable to do so because of their hatred toward him. They were unable because they were unwilling, and they were unwilling because of their hatred.

This truth can also be illustrated through the life of a political prisoner who has been incarcerated because of his animosity toward the throne. Imagine that out of the king's unmitigated mercy, he orders the cell doors open and offers the rebel full pardon if he will but merely acknowledge the king's right of sovereignty. However, driven by sheer hatred, the rebel slams the door shut and declares that he would rather rot in hell than bow the knee to the king. He had the capacity to hear the offer of pardon and understand it. The door was thrown open and a way was made. However the prisoner could not because he would not, and he would not because of his hatred for the king.

This is the way of the unregenerate person before God. He cannot come to God because he will not come to God, and he will not come because of his love for unrighteousness and his hatred for a holy and sovereign God. Thus, his heart can be compared to stone. It is lifeless and unresponsive to the call of the gospel apart from a supernatural work of the Spirit.

Some people say that the world would be converted if only we could give them a clearer vision of Jesus. However, such thinking demonstrates a superficial understanding of the depths of humanity's moral corruption, spiritual blindness, and hostility toward God. Imagine that we were able to draw open the curtains and present Jesus of Nazareth before an auditorium filled with unconverted people. How would they respond?

First, we would face the problem of their spiritual blindness. According to the Scriptures, they would not recognize the uniqueness of Christ's person or esteem the value of His teaching. In appearance, He would have no stately form or majesty that carnal people would look upon Him or be attracted to Him.[9] The Scriptures declare that His teaching would

---

9. Isaiah 53:2

be unacceptable to such people, that its truth would be indiscernible to them, and that they would denounce it as foolishness.[10] However, they are not victims of their ignorance, but rather they are the cause of it: professing to be wise, they have become fools.[11]

Second, if the spiritual blindness of these unconverted people were removed and they were able to see Christ and discern His teaching with greater clarity, we would still face an even more difficult problem: the moral corruption of their hearts and their hostility toward righteousness. The Bible teaches that people are radically depraved. They hate God and despise His righteous law. Therefore, the more these people discerned the true nature of Christ and the more they understood His teaching, the more they would hate Him. A greater revelation of the perfectly righteous Christ to unrighteous people will not draw them to Him, but rather drive them from Him. Jesus Himself said, "And this is the condemnation, that the light has come into the world, and men loved darkness rather than light, because their deeds were evil. For everyone practicing evil hates the light and does not come to the light, lest his deeds should be exposed" (John 3:19–20).

For an unconverted person to come to Christ, he must not only be given spiritual sight, but also his very nature must be changed. He must be transformed into a new creature that possesses new affections. Only then will he see Christ as He is and love the Christ he sees.

The magnitude of the change that must be wrought in a person before he is willing to come to Christ cannot be accomplished by force or the coercion of his will. It requires the supernatural recreating work of the Holy Spirit in regeneration. Imagine that a lone wolf has been raiding a flock of sheep. The shepherds band together and capture the animal. There are now three possible long-term solutions to the problem. First, the shepherds can kill the wolf and end its raids. Although the shepherds and the sheep will benefit from this course of action, it will provide very little benefit for the wolf. This represents a person under the judgment of God. Second, the shepherds can leave the wolf in a cage and keep it under guard for the rest of its life. The animal's behavior will be altered, but only because it is in the cage. It remains a killer, pacing back and forth in misery. It cannot deny its nature or break free

---

10. 1 Corinthians 2:14
11. Romans 1:22

from what it is. It longs to kill and eat. If left unattended, it would bolt from the cage and create as much carnage as possible. This represents the unconverted person under the bondage of religion. Again, while the wolf is in the cage, the shepherds and sheep benefit, but the wolf languishes in lust for sheep. The third solution is beyond the capacity and power of the shepherds. It is to transform the nature of the animal from a ravenous wolf to a docile sheep. Changing the nature of the wolf will change his affections toward both the shepherds and the sheep. He will follow the shepherd and live in harmony with the sheep. This represents the man regenerated by the power of the Holy Spirit. What is impossible with men is possible with God.[12]

Charles Spurgeon used the following illustration to demonstrate the true nature of the unconverted and the power of regeneration. Imagine that we place two dining options before a pig. On one side of the room, we set a table with the finest food available to us. On the other side, we place a trough of slop on the floor. The pig is then set free to choose the option it most desires. To the astonishment of city folk—but not to the farmer, who knows pigs—the specimen runs straight for the slop without giving the slightest thought to the lavish meal on the other side. It then plunges its head into the trough and eats with reckless abandon until its desires have been satisfied. It suffers no ailment from the refuse it has gulped down, and bears no shame before others for its behavior. In fact, it has acted in perfect conformity with its nature. It has done exactly what a pig should and will always do.

However, for the sake of argument, let's say that we have the power to change the nature of the swine and transform it into that of a human. What will be the result of this supernatural and ontological change? First, what the human had only moments before desired would now repulse him. The horrid smells that he had not noticed would become acute. Second, he would pull his head out of the trough and vomit up the filth for which he had previously hungered. There are some foods palatable to swine that the human stomach simply cannot bear. Third, he would realize that others had noticed his behavior. He would suffer the greatest shame and be most apologetic. Fourth, he would never forget the day of his transformation or cease to be repulsed by the shape of the trough or the smell of slop.

---

12. Luke 18:27

Though it may not be a pleasant contemplation, this illustration describes the conversion of every person who has ever truly come to Christ. The Scripture testifies that all of us were conceived in sin, and prior to conversion, we drank down iniquity like water.[13] Though God set His table before us and invited us to taste and see that the Lord is good, we cared nothing for His invitation.[14] All day He held out His hands to an obstinate people who chose the trough of this fallen world over the table set by God.[15] We ran to our moral filth as a pig runs to slop and mire. In doing so, we were acting in perfect conformity to what we were: radically depraved and morally corrupt. We had hearts of stone and were dead in our sins. We walked according to the course of this fallen world, even according to the will of the archenemy of God. We were driven by the lusts of our fallen natures, indulging the desires of the flesh, and were by nature children of wrath.[16]

Yet when all hope of any form of recuperation was lost, God intervened and raised us up in Christ to walk in newness of life.[17] He took out our heart of unresponsive stone and replaced it with a heart of living flesh. He changed our natures, and thus our affections and will. He recreated us in the image of God in true righteousness and holiness, and thus our palates changed, and we began to hunger and thirst for righteousness.[18]

As a result, we now hate the sin we once loved and love the righteousness we once hated. We are now ashamed of the rebellion of which we once boasted and glory in the God of whom we were once ashamed.[19] Though we are not immune to fleshly desires and the temptations of the filth we left behind, we now know the wrongness of them. If we are deceived and drawn to them again, we smell their foulness and taste their rot. Thus, we cannot tolerate them for long. Our very nature requires that we turn from them in disgust and repent in shame. We are new creatures with new affections that drive us back to God.

In conclusion, these truths leave us with some personal questions in two different categories. First, are we those who have merely made some

---

13. Job 15:16; Psalm 51:5
14. Psalm 34:8; Isaiah 55:1–2
15. Isaiah 65:2; Romans 10:21
16. Ephesians 2:1–3
17. Romans 6:5; Ephesians 2:4
18. Matthew 5:6; Ephesians 4:24
19. Romans 6:21

decision to accept Christ, or are we new creatures? Are we those who have simply joined ourselves to some expression or institution of Christianity, or have our hearts been changed? Is there any evidence to prove our boast of salvation? Have our affections been transformed? Have we become more responsive to the person and will of God? We would do well to remember the twin warnings the apostle Paul once gave: "For in Christ Jesus neither circumcision nor uncircumcision avails anything, but a new creation" (Gal. 6:15). For if anyone is in Christ, he is a new creature.[20]

Second, does our preaching to the unconverted or our methodology of evangelism correspond to what we know about the supernatural nature of conversion? If a person's salvation depends merely upon the manipulation of his will or emotions, then there are countless ways to bring him to a proper decision. But if a person's conversion requires a supernatural work of the Spirit on par with the creation of the universe and the resurrection of Christ from the dead, then we know that all the convincing, coercion, and manipulation in the world are not enough to bring about the desired end. We must put away the fleshly arsenal of eloquence, clever arguments, and manipulative invitations.[21] We must see people as bones that are very dry and as those who have no possibility of life apart from a direct and personal work of God. In all we do, we must defer to the power of God alone.[22] We must stake the whole of our ministries upon the biblical fact that the gospel is the power of God unto salvation, and we must preach it with the greatest confidence, clarity, and boldness.[23]

Every time we preach to the people of this world, we must see ourselves as Ezekiel walking in the valley of dry bones.[24] If we are asked, "Can these bones live?" we must defer to the sovereignty and strength of God alone. The might that is required for the resurrection that is needed is beyond human power, and it is not effected by the will of man. The wind blows where it wishes, and we hear the sound of it, but God alone

---

20. 2 Corinthians 5:17

21. 1 Corinthians 2:1–2

22. "The hand of the LORD came upon me and brought me out in the Spirit of the LORD, and set me down in the midst of the valley; and it was full of bones. Then He caused me to pass by them all around, and behold, there were very many in the open valley; and indeed they were very dry. And He said to me, 'Son of man, can these bones live?' So I answered, 'O Lord GOD, You know'" (Ezek. 37:1–3).

23. Romans 1:16

24. Ezekiel 37:1–10

knows where it comes from or where it is going.[25] Nevertheless, by faith we must stand and prophesy over these bones and say to them, "O dry bones, hear the word of the LORD."[26] We must cry out in prayer to the Wind, that He might come and breathe on these slain so that they might come to life. Although we must draw upon the gifts that have been given to us, we must be careful to strip ourselves of all the armaments of the flesh. We must confine ourselves to the preaching of the gospel, because it is the power of God unto salvation and the means by which the Spirit of God raises the dead and converts the sinner.[27]

---

25. Ezekiel 37:3; John 3:8
26. Ezekiel 37:4
27. Romans 1:16

CHAPTER TEN

The Effectual Spirit

I will put My Spirit within you and cause you to walk in My statutes, and you will keep My judgments and do them. Then you shall dwell in the land that I gave to your fathers; you shall be My people, and I will be your God.

—Ezekiel 36:27–28

Having considered regeneration's work in the human heart, we will turn our attention to the Holy Spirit's indwelling of the believer and its results. Once again, as we read Ezekiel 36:27–28, we are confronted with the absolute certainty of the one who is speaking. His words exude an air of sovereignty and power. He has a plan for the full redemption of His people, and He will see to its completion for His glory and their good. He will call forth a people, change their natures, and indwell them with His Spirit. In return, they will be His people, and He will be their God. They will walk in His statutes and be careful to observe His ordinances. They will possess the inheritance that He has prepared for them from before the foundation of the world.[1] The apostle Paul writes to the church in Ephesus, "In Him also we have obtained an inheritance, being predestined according to the purpose of Him who works all things according to the counsel of His will" (Eph. 1:11).

The mystery and grandeur of divine providence is unsearchable. An eternity of study will not reveal all of its truths. If the world were filled to the brim with the greatest discourses on the subject, there would still be more to discover. However, what we do know is that God will lead His people to their appointed destination, and He will not lose even one among the multitude. He who began a good work in them will perfect it.[2]

---

1. Matthew 25:34; Ephesians 1:4
2. Philippians 1:6

And yet they will each come freely, following the desires of their renewed hearts, without divine coercion or the slightest infringement upon their wills. He will make them obedient by making them new. He will change their behavior by changing their heart. "If anyone is in Christ, he is a new creation" (2 Cor. 5:17). "Oh, the depth of the riches both of the wisdom and knowledge of God! How unsearchable are His judgments and His ways past finding out!" (Rom. 11:33).

THE INDWELLING SPIRIT

In the previous chapter, we learned that God promised to create a new people for Himself through the supernatural regenerating work of the Holy Spirit. He would remove their spiritually dead and radically depraved heart that was hostile toward Him and set against His will and put in its place a new and living heart, recreated in the image of God.[3] This new heart would be alive to God, would respond positively to divine stimuli, and would manifest a "new spirit," or inward disposition, toward God that would both esteem Him and delight in His law.

In this text, we will see that at conversion God not only transforms our natures and our spirit, or disposition, toward Him, but He also indwells us with His Spirit. He does this so that He might both ensure and complete the work that He has begun: "I will put My Spirit within you and cause you to walk in My statutes." Based on this truth and those we discussed in the previous chapter, we can create this outline to describe God's magnificent work of conversion in the life of every believer.

- *I will give you a new heart*—God regenerates the believer's heart and changes his nature; he becomes a new creature.[4] This is the reality of every Christian, without exception.

- *I will put a new spirit within you*—This is the result of regeneration. A new creature recreated in the image of God has a new spirit or inward disposition toward God. He possesses new affections that delight in God and His law.[5]

---

3. Ezekiel 36:26
4. Ezekiel 36:26
5. Ezekiel 36:26

- *I will put My Spirit within you*—God indwells the believer through the Holy Spirit to instruct, prompt, and empower him to walk according to His statutes.[6]

These three simple statements reveal both the wisdom and power of God in our salvation. Even the slightest contemplation and understanding of them should create in us the greatest confidence and joy. We were dead in trespasses and sin, haters of God, suppressers of truth, and hostile to righteousness.[7] We were without strength and unable to affect reconciliation with God or to free ourselves from the power of sin.[8] We were without hope and without God in the world.[9] Nevertheless, what is impossible for men is possible for God.[10] For the glory of His name and the good of His people, He has designed and decreed our salvation. It was figured in His mind before the foundation of the world, and it was made a reality in our time through the incarnation of His Son and the sending forth of the Holy Spirit. Through the bloody death of Christ, He has provided for His people's reconciliation. Through the regenerating work of the Spirit, He changes their hearts and consequently transforms their affections. He indwells them with His Spirit and prompts and empowers them to obey. He does all of this to the praise of the glory of His grace, that it might be to Him a name of joy, praise, and glory before all the nations of the earth, which will hear of all the good that He will do for them.[11]

This inward work of God on behalf of His people has an amazing parallel in the book of Psalms, where David cries out:

> Create in me a clean heart, O God,
> And renew a steadfast spirit within me.
> Do not cast me away from Your presence,
> And do not take Your Holy Spirit from me.
> Restore to me the joy of Your salvation,
> And uphold me by Your generous Spirit (51:10–12).

In this text, David has committed a great sin against God and been brought to repentance. In seeking restoration, he recognizes his two

---

6. Ezekiel 36:27
7. Romans 1:18; 1:30; 8:7; Ephesians 2:1
8. Romans 5:6; 7:24; 8:7
9. Ephesians 2:12
10. Matthew 19:26; Mark 10:27; Luke 18:27
11. Jeremiah 33:9; Ephesians 1:6

greatest needs. First, David asks God to renew a steadfast spirit within him, an inner disposition that is steadfast in faith toward God and able to resist the temptations that would again assail him. Second, he asks that the Holy Spirit might continue to indwell him and sustain his spirit in its renewed state that he might not fall back into willful disobedience.

The truth we should learn from this is that to accomplish the work of salvation in the life of the Christian, two things are necessary: the initial regeneration of the heart and its ongoing preservation. At conversion, a person is given a new heart, resulting in a new spirit or inward disposition toward God. However, the ongoing work of the Spirit of God, who indwells him, must continually sustain, uphold, and strengthen him. This is the believer's great and ongoing need, and it has been met in every sense by God's wisdom, power, and graciousness. He not only creates a right spirit within us through the work of the Holy Spirit in regeneration, but He indwells us with His Spirit to ensure that the work will continue and progress until that final day.

God's complementary works of creation and providence are a helpful illustration of this truth. God not only created the universe, but He must continue to sustain it.[12] He not only is the origin of all life, but He must continue to give life to all things.[13] If God withdrew His Spirit, all flesh would perish and every person would return to dust.[14] In a similar fashion, God must not only regenerate us and make us a new creation, but He must also sustain the new creation that He has made. God must not only put a new spirit within us, but He must also sustain that new spirit through the Holy Spirit that He has made to indwell us. To put it simply, God must not only save a person, but He must also sustain him in that salvation.

The purpose of pointing out this truth is to magnify the power of God in salvation and to show that the true Christian will progress in sanctification and bear fruit. However, in this truth is also a wonderful and necessary practical application for the Christian life: the believer is utterly dependent upon the life-sustaining work of the Holy Spirit. There is so much dangerous heresy within the evangelical community

---

12. Genesis 1:1–2; Job 12:10; 34:14–15; Psalm 104:27–30; John 1:2–3; Colossians 1:17; Hebrews 1:3

13. 1 Timothy 6:13

14. Job 34:14–15

regarding the Holy Spirit that many sincere Christians have almost withdrawn themselves from even a proper consideration of His role in the Christian life. However, we must remember that His person and ministry are indispensable. It is impossible to live the Christian life apart from Him. For the believer's continued growth and fruitfulness, he must recognize this truth and cultivate a life of absolute dependence upon His person, wisdom, and power. Like the Galatians, we must be reminded that Christian life that began by the Spirit cannot be perfected in the flesh.[15] As justification is from faith to faith, so sanctification begins and ends with the person and work of the Holy Spirit.[16]

THE CORRESPONDING RESULTS

As with all the promises and works of God in the believer's life, there are corresponding results. Through the prophet Ezekiel, God promises to put His Spirit within us. Then, with the greatest confidence in His own power, He promises that such an indwelling will result in a new life marked by obedience to His will: "I will put My Spirit within you and cause you to walk in My statutes, and you will keep My judgments and do them" (Ezek. 36:27).

The word *cause* is translated from a Hebrew verb that denotes causation that may also be translated "to make" or "to move."[17] The idea Ezekiel is communicating is that through the indwelling Spirit, God will cause His people to walk in His statutes and be careful to observe His ordinances. Although David uses a different Hebrew verb in Psalm 119:35, he is communicating this same idea: "Make me walk in the path of Your commandments, for I delight in it."

That God will make or cause His children to walk in His commands is an undeniable biblical truth, and therefore requires no defense. However, the manner in which He accomplishes this work does deserve further explanation. From the outset, we must affirm unequivocally that God does not violate the will of His people or move them to obedience through any measure of coercion. He does not gain their compliance against their will or contrary to their affections. Rather, at conversion, God regenerates the heart of the believer and transforms his affections. Thus, he becomes

---

15. Galatians 3:3
16. Romans 1:17
17. Hebrew: *'asah.*

a new creature with a new nature that no longer lusts for what is contrary to the will of God, but his delight is in the law of the Lord.[18] Concurrently, God indwells the believer with the Holy Spirit, who continues to teach, lead, renew, and empower him to walk in submission to the will of God throughout the course of his earthly pilgrimage. The believer will still be buffeted by countless temptations and pained by many sins; he will always be in need of grace. However, godly affections and the empowering of the Spirit will mark the life of the true believer and enable him to walk in regular or consistent obedience to God. Although God does ensure the obedience of His people, He does not bring His people kicking and screaming into submission; rather, they follow Him as a sheep follows its shepherd. As Jesus declared to the unbelieving Jews: "My sheep hear My voice, and I know them, and they follow Me" (John 10:27).

FOUR COMMON SCENARIOS

To illustrate these truths and demonstrate their application, we will consider four scenarios that commonly occur in the modern evangelical community. The first three cases involve individuals who would identify themselves as Christians but whose experience bears little or no resemblance to conversion as it is set forth in the text. The fourth involves a person who has been born again and demonstrates the fruit of it.

The first case involves an individual who has made a decision to accept Christ and yet shows little interest in the things of God and bears no apparent fruit other than his confession of faith. To address his disinterest in his newfound faith and his lack of commitment, the church assigns him an accountability partner and enrolls him in a follow-up program. The dedicated Christian assigned to the task is very diligent, but he makes little progress. After several visits and phone calls, he is able to bring the new convert to a Sunday morning service. After a few more months of relentless pursuit, the new convert is baptized and victory is declared. However, without constant prodding, the new convert falls back into apathy and eventually disappears altogether. He is like King Joash, who did what was right in the sight of the Lord during the days of Jehoiada the priest but forsook the Lord as soon as Jehoiada died.[19]

---

18. Psalm 1:2; 1 John 5:3
19. 2 Chronicles 24:2, 17–18

He shows little evidence of regeneration, a new heart, or new affections. Another's constant prodding moved him, but he did not follow willingly as a sheep that hears and obeys the Shepherd's voice.

The second case involves an individual who attends a contemporary church service known for its entertaining worship, cutting-edge media presentations, and short sermons emphasizing life principles for the real world. The individual enjoys the services, develops interesting relationships with others, and gains a sense of belonging. His felt needs are being met as never before, and his life has a sense of purpose. However, in such a setting, the gospel and Christ's radical call to costly discipleship rarely confront him. In turn, he demonstrates little passion for the knowledge of God or the application of the Scriptures to his daily life. Little separates his purpose, thoughts, and deeds from that of the secular culture that surrounds him. So has he been drawn to Christ, or to a social group that affirms his worth and meets his felt needs? Have his affections been transformed so that he esteems the worth of Christ above all things, or has he merely found a place and people that enhance his present life?

The third case involves an individual who once professed Christ but has not been in fellowship with the church for years. The new pastor visits him and finds him both cordial and apologetic. During the course of their conversation, the pastor confronts him with regard to his worldliness, fruitless life, and neglect of the church. In response, he agrees with the verdict leveled against him. He admits that he should give up all his vices regardless of the pleasure they afford him, discipline himself to turn away from the sin that attracts him, and just do the right thing. By some appearances, it may seem that God has done a work in his heart, but a closer examination reveals that his heart and affections have remained the same. In fact, his own words are an indictment against him. He has simply made the decision to turn away from all the wicked things he still loves and do all the righteous things he still hates in order to save himself from judgment and secure his home in heaven![20] However, he is not, in reality, a true child of God. Although the Christian will struggle with temptation and the desires of the flesh that war against him, he will exhibit a noticeable transformation in his desires that will continue growing throughout the course of his life. He does not turn from sin

---

20. I first heard this truth in a discussion with Pastor Charles Leiter of Lake Road Chapel in Kirksville, Missouri.

merely because it is the right thing to do, nor does he practice goodness for goodness's sake. Rather, he begins to truly hate the sin that God hates and love the righteousness that God loves. He is not driven by mere duty, but also by his godly affections that flow from a regenerated heart.

The fourth case involves an individual who hears the gospel and makes a profession of faith in Christ. He is not sure what has happened to him or how to explain it. He just knows that something is very different—that he is different. He begins to see his former life in a new light. The things in which he once delighted—and even boasted—seem wrong and shameful to him. He begins to take interest in Christ and wants to know more about Him and His will. He seems estranged from his old friends and finds better company among the saints. As he continues on, he experiences progress in his growth to maturity, but he also faces challenges and all-too-frequent failures. He delights in the will of God but finds that he is not immune to temptation. He battles against the world on the outside and the flesh within. He rejoices in the grace of God that enables him to overcome and laments the times he fails. He finds in himself a great contradiction. He listens to sermons and reads books that cause him to delight in Christ as the end of all desire, and then a few moments later he must struggle with a lukewarm heart. When he reads the Word, he receives great consolation, but it also pierces him like a two-edged sword and exposes sin that was before unknown. As he progresses further in his pilgrimage, he becomes acutely aware of God's paternal control of his life. Sometimes the discipline is slight, but at other times, it seems as if he is being scourged without relief. A few times, he even thinks of walking away, but he cannot. He cannot bear just the thought of being separated from Christ, and so he returns, "weak and wounded, sick and sore."[21] It seems to him that the Christian life is three steps forward and two steps back. He sins, but he cannot continue in his sin; he falls, but he cannot remain fallen. He seems to climb one hill just to go down the other side. However, little by little, he is ascending, progressing, and growing. In all this, the good and bad, is inescapable evidence of conversion. All true believers are able to identify with this scenario.

To conclude this chapter, we must all consider this question: Is there evidence that God has changed our natures and transformed our affections? Is there evidence of the indwelling of the Holy Spirit that teaches,

---

21. Joseph Hart, "Come, Ye Sinners, Poor and Needy," stanza 1.

leads, and empowers us to walk in God's statutes and be careful to observe His will? If we are ever to understand the nature and power of conversion, we must first come to terms with this great truth: God does not merely save a person from the condemnation of sin and then leave him without the divine aid necessary to overcome its power. Rather, He provides all that is necessary to ensure that His people will walk in His statutes and be careful to observe His will.

PART THREE

New People and the Nature of True Conversion

But this is the covenant that I will make with the house of Israel after those days, says the LORD: I will put My law in their minds, and write it on their hearts; and I will be their God, and they shall be My people. No more shall every man teach his neighbor, and every man his brother, saying, "Know the LORD," for they all shall know Me, from the least of them to the greatest of them, says the LORD. For I will forgive their iniquity, and their sin I will remember no more.　—Jeremiah 31:33–34

They shall be My people, and I will be their God; then I will give them one heart and one way, that they may fear Me forever, for the good of them and their children after them. And I will make an everlasting covenant with them, that I will not turn away from doing them good; but I will put My fear in their hearts so that they will not depart from Me. Yes, I will rejoice over them to do them good, and I will assuredly plant them in this land, with all My heart and with all My soul.　—Jeremiah 32:38–42

CHAPTER ELEVEN

The Glory of the New Covenant

Behold, the days are coming, says the LORD, when I will make a new covenant with the house of Israel and with the house of Judah—not according to the covenant that I made with their fathers in the day that I took them by the hand to lead them out of the land of Egypt, My covenant which they broke, though I was a husband to them, says the LORD. But this is the covenant that I will make with the house of Israel after those days, says the LORD: I will put My law in their minds, and write it on their hearts.

—Jeremiah 31:31–33

In our study of Ezekiel 36:22–28, we considered some of the marks of regeneration and conversion as set forth in the new covenant promises of the Old Testament. From this text, we gained insight into two important truths. First, we learned that conversion is a supernatural work of God to be compared with the creation of the universe and the resurrection of Jesus Christ from the dead.[1] A miraculous work of God transforms a person's nature and affections, causes him to keep God's commands, and makes him careful to observe His ordinances. It is a sure work of God that He begins and perfects by His Spirit and for His glory. It is for His sake that He began the work, and it is for His glorious name that He will see it through.

Second, we learned that there is a great contrast between the scriptural view of conversion and that of contemporary evangelicalism. Today's gospel has been reduced to little more than a set of spiritual laws, and even the most essential doctrines associated with biblical and historic evangelism have been neglected. Preachers call people to "make a

---

1. 2 Corinthians 5:21; Ephesians 2:5–6

decision" or pray a prayer, and they make little mention of the biblical demands of repentance and faith and show little concern for their proper understanding. They welcome those who "make a decision" for Christ into the family of God and give them little examination or warning. Few ever learn about the evidences of genuine conversion or receive instruction about examining themselves in light of the Scriptures to determine if they truly are in the faith.[2] Finally, many kinds of methodologies and programs of discipleship are employed in order to make so-called carnal Christians grow in their faith. Even in light of the overwhelming failure of these programs to produce a vibrant Christianity, few are willing to entertain the possibility that the great multitude of "carnal Christians" in the church are simply unconverted.

As we consider Jeremiah 31:31–33, we will seek to understand further the nature of conversion and the characteristics of a genuine Christian. We will begin by comparing and contrasting the nation of Israel under the old covenant with the church of Jesus Christ under the new. From this, we will learn that the nation of Israel, which consisted of the physical descendants of Abraham, was largely an unregenerate nation with only a small remnant of believers, or true Israelites. For this reason, idolatry, rebellion, and apostasy mark Israel's history. In contrast, the church of Jesus Christ consists of the spiritual descendants of Abraham, both Jews and Gentiles. Every true member of the church has been regenerated by the Holy Spirit and has received the law of God—not on tablets of stone—but written on their hearts. For this reason, devotion, obedience, and perseverance mark the true church, even under the most terrible circumstances.

THE WEAKNESS OF THE OLD COVENANT

Jeremiah 31:31 begins with the interjection *behold*, indicating that God is calling Israel's attention to something of utmost importance, something that stands out even from the inspired text that surrounds it. He is going to make an announcement of unmitigated importance. Therefore, all lesser activity must cease, every conversation should stop, and every ear must strain toward the words God will speak.

Having called Israel to attention, God now directs their gaze to the future, when He would make a new covenant with them that would far

---

2. 2 Corinthians 13:5

surpass the one He had made with them when He delivered them out of Egypt. Though the old covenant He made with Israel at Sinai was also marked by grace, despite its strictness, rigor, and ethnic limitations, the old trappings of the economy were to be done away with in Christ. To the contemporary reader, God's announcement of this new covenant does not seem monumental, but to the Israelites to whom the message was first delivered, it was nothing short of earthshaking. Israel and her entire history as a nation was based upon the covenant made at Sinai. Even to suggest that it was to be done away with and replaced by another was to predict an event of cataclysmic proportions. It meant that the very foundation of Israel's existence and relationship with God was to be replaced by another. It was more than a paradigm shift. It was tantamount to saying that reality would be done away with, and something else would be put in its place.

Again, unless we grasp the radical nature of Jeremiah's announcement, we can never understand the superiority of the new covenant over the old, the nature of the church, or the nature of true conversion. Through the prophet Jeremiah, God was promising to do a work of salvation among His people that eye had not seen and ear had not heard nor had previously entered into the heart of man, a work that would be exceeding abundantly beyond all that one might ever ask or think.[3]

After making such a startling announcement, God turns to expose the weaknesses of the old covenant, which were not due to any blight in God's character or failure in His providence. Rather, the weakness of the old covenant was entirely due to man and his fallenness. As the apostle Paul writes, "Let God be true but every man a liar. As it is written: 'That You may be justified in Your words, and may overcome when You are judged'" (Rom. 3:4).

God begins His dismantling of the old covenant by setting forth His work of redemption and faithfulness to the nation of Israel. He had taken them by the hand and led them out of the land of Egypt. He had entered into a covenant with them as a husband would a bride. He had cared for Israel and her needs in an exemplary manner. However, Israel had not responded in kind; rather, she had become the kind of bride so glaringly illustrated in the relationship between Hosea and Gomer. She was a wife of harlotry.[4] She had broken God's covenant as a wayward bride

---

3. 1 Corinthians 2:9; Ephesians 3:20
4. Hosea 1:2

might spurn the love of a faithful husband and shame him through her frequent adulteries. Repeatedly, she had run from Him into the arms of another. Repeatedly, He had faithfully retrieved her until He finally banished her into exile. Though He had longed to be her God and for her to be His people, she had rarely complied.

Israel's constant rebellion brings us to an important truth. Under the old covenant, God made Israel to be His people, yet we must not think that they were all Israel who were descended from Israel.[5] The Israel that came out of Egypt was made up of the physical descendants of Abraham, but that does not mean they were all believers. In fact, the biblical account proves just the opposite. Although there was a godly remnant, a small minority, in the nation who were truly regenerate and justified by faith, the great majority were unregenerate and unbelieving idolaters. The writer of Hebrews tells us that the vast majority of those that came out of Egypt led by Moses died in the wilderness because of their unbelief.[6] Even in the time of the kings, the remnant of true believers in Israel was so small that Elijah cried out, "LORD, they have killed Your prophets and torn down Your altars, and I alone am left" (Rom. 11:3; cf. 1 Kings 19:10, 14). God's response to the discouraged prophet not only proved that a remnant had remained, but that it was indeed very small in comparison to the number of the sons of Israel. He declared, "I have reserved for Myself seven thousand men who have not bowed the knee to Baal" (Rom. 11:4; cf. 1 Kings 19:18). This tragic reality seems to mark most of Israel's history. Even the coming of Christ revealed that only a few believing or true Israelites remained who were "just and devout" and "looked for redemption in Jerusalem" (Luke 2:25, 38).

This truth about the nature of Israel under the old covenant is important because too often the rebellious behavior of the nation of Israel has been used to justify the same behavior in the so-called professing church.[7] It is argued that the overwhelming carnality in the church and the existence of only a small godly remnant is to be expected because that is exactly what we see when we study the history of Israel. However, as we shall see, the comparison between Israel and the church is wrong.

---

5. Romans 9:6

6. Hebrews 3:16–19

7. The term *professing church* references all those who profess faith in Jesus Christ and identify themselves with Christianity. The *professing church* and the *true church of Jesus Christ* are not synonymous terms.

The whole point of the new covenant is that it would not be like the old. In the old covenant, God called a physical nation descended from Abraham to be His people, but within that great multitude of individuals, only a small number of them were truly regenerate and believing. The rest were unregenerate and carnal, and are now suffering eternal perdition. In the new covenant, God is calling forth a spiritual nation made up of Jews and Gentiles, and all of them are regenerate and believing. There is not a godly remnant in the true church; that true church is the godly remnant.

The Scriptures teach that there will always be believers and unbelievers mixed in the professing church.[8] We also understand from the Scriptures and from church history that this harmful state will become more prominent when the church preaches something less than a biblical gospel and neglects church discipline. Nevertheless, the true church is made up of only those who are regenerate, repenting, and believing and who are being conformed to Christ's image. This is the major difference between the old and new covenants, and we must maintain and proclaim it.

THE GLORY OF THE NEW COVENANT

On Mount Sinai, God carved the Decalogue, or Ten Commandments, on tablets of stone, and He gave them to the people of Israel through the mediation of Moses.[9] The Scriptures record the event in the following manner: "And when [God] had made an end of speaking with him on Mount Sinai, He gave Moses two tablets of the Testimony, tablets of stone, written with the finger of God" (Ex. 31:18).

The law was God's great gift to Israel, and it should have benefited the nation in every way.[10] However, as soon as God gave the law, the people broke it. As Moses was receiving the law upon Sinai, the people made for themselves a molten calf and worshiped it as the god who had brought them out of the land of Egypt.[11] Having broken the first two of the ten commands, they then further corrupted themselves by every

---

8. Matthew 13:24–30, 36–43

9. *Decalogue* comes from the Greek word *dekalogos* (*deka* [ten] + *logos* [word]). Therefore, the Decalogue is often referred to as the "Ten Words."

10. Romans 3:1–2

11. Exodus 32:1–5

form of immorality.[12] As the Scriptures declare, "The people sat down to eat and drink, and rose up to play" (Ex. 32:6–7).

In response to this great rebellion, Moses threw down the tablets and shattered them at the foot of the mountain.[13] What God gave to Israel for life became for them a catalyst of condemnation and death.[14] Eventually, the unbelief of the people and their constant rejection of God's commands led to their near total annihilation in the wilderness. The author of Hebrews writes, "Now with whom was [God] angry forty years? Was it not with those who sinned, whose corpses fell in the wilderness?" (3:17).

In this tragic, yet often repeated rebellion of the nation of Israel, three important truths become clear. First, the divine origin and nature of the law is clearly revealed. It was not a human or angelic invention; God wrote it. Moses testified, "Now the tablets were the work of God, and the writing was the writing of God engraved on the tablets" (Ex. 32:16). Since the law finds its origin in God, it is a trustworthy expression of His righteousness and wisdom. In the words of the apostle Paul, "Therefore the law is holy, and the commandment holy and just and good" (Rom. 7:12). Therefore, we may be confident that the weakness of the old covenant had nothing to do with some fault in the law. The law was unable to bring life to the nation of Israel because of the weakness of fallen human flesh.[15]

Second, the law was carved upon tablets of stone taken from the mountain of God. The stone not only represents the immutable nature of the law, but it also represents the nature of the hearts to which God gave it. The vast majority of the Israelites were "dead in trespasses and sins," and their hearts were as hard as stone (Eph. 2:1). Although the Holy Spirit had regenerated a small remnant of true believers' hearts, the rest were like the pagans that surrounded them. They were "stiff-necked and uncircumcised in heart," and "they made their hearts like flint, refusing to hear the law" (Acts 7:51; Zech. 7:12).

The law was written upon tablets of stone, but not upon the hearts of most Israelites. Though it was given *to* all of them, it was never *in* many of them. For the majority, it was always external and foreign, as something contrary to their nature and in opposition to their desires. They had no

---

12. Exodus 20:3–6
13. Exodus 32:19
14. Deuteronomy 30:15, 19; Romans 7:9–10
15. Romans 8:3

affinity for the law, no spontaneous or natural affection for it. Instead, they hated it and kicked against it. Because of their stony hearts, the Ten Words of the law resulted in ten indictments against them, and what was meant for life procured their death.[16] This is why the prophet Ezekiel looked forward to the day when the Holy Spirit would replace these unmovable hearts of stone with hearts of responsive flesh.[17]

Third, the law, the old covenant, was mediated through Moses. Though he was an exemplary man, he was still a man fraught with all the sins and weaknesses of his people. Although he was faithful over God's house as a servant, he had no power to atone for sin or to procure any lasting or inward transformation of those who followed him out of Egypt.[18] It is impossible for the blood of bulls and goats to take away sins or make the worshiper perfect in conscience.[19] It is impossible for the law, due to the weakness of human flesh, to change a person's affections and transform him in thought and deed.[20] It is for this reason that God declares through Jeremiah the joyful news of a new and superior covenant established upon better promises.[21] It would possess and display a fullness of which the old covenant was only a type or shadow. It would make demands upon the people of God that far exceeded what Moses handed down to them, and yet it would provide a transformation and power that would enable them to obey. The law would no longer be written upon tablets of stone, imposed upon hearts of stone, and result in condemnation and death. In the new covenant, God would take away the iniquity of His people through one greater than Moses; transform their hearts into living, responsive flesh; and write His law upon them.[22]

When God declares through Jeremiah, "I will put My law within them, and on their heart I will write it," He is speaking of the wonderful doctrine of regeneration. In the new covenant, God would not merely impose His law upon an unwilling people, but He would recreate that people and make them fit for such a law. It would be as we have already considered in the prophecies of Ezekiel. God would take out His people's

---

16. Romans 7:9–10
17. Ezekiel 36:26
18. Hebrews 3:5
19. Hebrews 9:9; 10:4
20. Romans 8:3
21. Hebrews 8:6
22. Hebrews 3:1–3

hearts of stone and replace them with hearts of responsive flesh. They would no longer be a people antagonistic to God or contrary to His law, but rather would be willing, obedient, and devout. In other words, through the regenerating work of the Holy Spirit, God would restore His image in His people. He would change their natures, and, as a result, they would possess new affections. Correspondingly, He would write His law upon their hearts with indelible ink. His stylus would be the finger of God. Then, to insure the work and promote it to its desired end, He would indwell His people with the Holy Spirit and cause them to walk in His statutes and to be careful to keep His ordinances.[23]

It is important that we understand that the language employed here is not exaggerated poetic prose, meant only to enliven the heart. What God promised through the new covenant is now a living reality in the true church of Jesus Christ. Every true member of the body of Christ is a supernatural recreation of the Spirit of God. Each has undergone a radical transformation in the very core of his being and has the law of God written on his heart. To those in the new covenant, the law is no longer an external code contrary to their natures and opposed by them. Instead, it has become a part of them. It is no longer a burden, but a delight. It is no longer a catalyst for their condemnation and death, but an effective guide to greater godliness.

This good news in no way discounts the fact that the individual believer and the collective church are still awaiting their full and final glorification. Even the most devout believer is still fraught with many weaknesses and failures that he will not overcome until the return of Christ and the consummation of all things. Nevertheless, a new relationship to God and His will marks the true Christian and the true church. In the new covenant, rebellion and disobedience are no longer the prominent marks of God's people. Instead, their outstanding feature is their new affection for God, His Son, and His commands. Psalm 119 describes the new affections beautifully:

> And I will delight myself in Your commandments,
> Which I love.
> My hands also I will lift up to Your commandments,
> Which I love,
> And I will meditate on Your statutes (vv. 47–48).

---

23. Ezekiel 36:26–27

Your testimonies I have taken as a heritage forever,
For they are the rejoicing of my heart.
I have inclined my heart to perform Your statutes
Forever, to the very end (vv. 111–12).

Therefore I love Your commandments
More than gold, yes, than fine gold!
Therefore all Your precepts concerning all things
I consider to be right;
I hate every false way (vv. 127–28).

It is unsound hermeneutically and extremely dangerous to use the almost constant rebellion of Israel to justify the near constant rebellion of the so-called carnal Christian and the professing church. The rampant rebellion in much of Western evangelicalism is not because the new covenant is no better than the old is or because it shares some of the same weaknesses. On the contrary, apathy, materialism, and rebellion have occurred because many who profess Christ are not really of Christ, and much of what is called the church is not the true, living church at all. We have reduced the gospel of Christ and its demands; we have dressed the church to look like the world; we have refused to preach costly grace or separation from that which defiles; and we have all but disdained any form of censure or church discipline. For these reasons and more, numerous individuals make a claim to Christianity without any of its accompanying evidences, and ecclesiastical organizations proudly identify themselves as the church, yet bear little resemblance to the bride of Christ as she is revealed in the New Testament.

We must therefore return to a biblical understanding of regeneration and conversion. We must deny the popular rhetoric that portrays the church as primarily a collection of saved but carnal people with only a tiny remnant of spiritual or devout followers of Christ within its midst. We must once again cry out, "Ye must be born again!" and we must explain that such a new birth will result in a transformed heart that delights in the law that has been written on it by the very finger of God.

CHAPTER TWELVE

The Making of New People

I will be their God, and they shall be My people.
—Jeremiah 31:33

When God declares through Jeremiah, "I will put My law within them, and on their heart I will write it," He is speaking of the work of regeneration. When He declares, "I will be their God, and they shall be My people," He is speaking of the result of that work: a unique relationship between God and a community of people who would believe on His name and walk according to His commands. Not only would this new covenant people be obedient to God's law, but also they would possess a marked devotion and fidelity to God Himself. They would have an affinity—a natural and spontaneous affection—for Him, and He would claim them as His own. He would be their God in truth and righteousness, and they would be a people who would worship Him in spirit and in truth; such people God seeks to be His worshipers.[1]

GOD'S LONGING FOR A PEOPLE

Since the fall and throughout all of Scripture, God's purpose in redemption has been to make a people for Himself out of the great mass of fallen humanity. To Abraham He said, "Also I give to you and your descendants after you the land in which you are a stranger, all the land of Canaan, as an everlasting possession; and I will be their God" (Gen. 17:8). To Moses He promised, "I will dwell among the children of Israel and will be their God," and, "I will walk among you and be your God, and you shall be My people" (Ex. 29:45; Lev. 26:12).

---

1. Zechariah 8:8; John 4:23

God promised the most intimate fellowship to the nation of Israel; however, they seldom responded in a worthy or appropriate manner, so the prophets often severely rebuked them. Isaiah declared that an ox knows its owner, and a donkey its master's manger, but Israel did not understand the worth of God or esteem their relationship with Him.[2] The prophet Malachi argued that in the natural course of things, a son honors his father, and a servant his master, but Israel did not honor God or demonstrate reverence toward Him. Instead, the nation despised His name and rejected His commands.[3] Recorded in the book of Nehemiah is a corporate confession in which the nation of Israel acknowledges their longstanding disobedience and rebellion against God: they had cast His law behind their backs and killed His prophets who admonished them to return.[4] Although God had made a covenant with them and revealed Himself to them in an unprecedented manner, the Scriptures describe them as "stiff-necked and uncircumcised in heart" and "always [resisting] the Holy Spirit" (Acts 7:51). Such obstinate rebellion grieved the heart of God and resulted in the following divine exclamation: "Oh, that they had such a heart in them that they would fear Me and always keep all My commandments, that it might be well with them and with their children forever!" (Deut. 5:29).

From the outset of His covenant with Israel, God longed for a people that would esteem His worth and keep His commandments in order that He might bless them and establish them forever. Then, as we turn the pages of the Old Testament, we see this divine longing become a clearly defined promise. The God who works everything after the counsel of His will would carry out His desire upon the earth.[5] He would get for Himself a people who would take Him as their God. He would circumcise their heart of stone, create in them a new heart, and make them responsive to His will. So we learn from the following prophesies taken from Jeremiah and Ezekiel:

> Then I will give them a heart to know Me, that I am the LORD; and they shall be My people, and I will be their God, for they shall return to Me with their whole heart (Jer. 24:7).

---

2. Isaiah 1:3
3. Malachi 1:6
4. Nehemiah 9:26
5. Ephesians 1:11

Thus says the Lord God: "Surely I will take the children of Israel from among the nations, wherever they have gone, and will gather them from every side and bring them into their own land; and I will make them one nation in the land, on the mountains of Israel; and one king shall be king over them all; they shall no longer be two nations, nor shall they ever be divided into two kingdoms again. They shall not defile themselves anymore with their idols, nor with their detestable things, nor with any of their transgressions; but I will deliver them from all their dwelling places in which they have sinned, and will cleanse them. Then they shall be My people, and I will be their God.

"David My servant shall be king over them, and they shall all have one shepherd; they shall also walk in My judgments and observe My statutes, and do them" (Ezek. 37:21–24).

From the beginning, God longed for a people, but all were unfit for the task, proving that the answer is not found in man, but in God's wisdom, sovereignty, and power. What is impossible for men is possible for God![6] To make a people for Himself out of a fallen and morally corrupt humanity would require nothing short of a miracle equal to the creation of the universe. The Spirit of God who hovered over a formless void in the making of the world would hover over the heart of every member of God's new people, resurrecting and recreating them from a depraved and loathsome mass of humanity into the children of the living God.[7]

GOD'S LONGING FULFILLED

Although this work may seem too marvelous to believe, it is exactly what God promises in the new covenant and the individual Christian and the collective true church live out every day. Through the atoning work of Christ and the regenerating work of the Holy Spirit, God has made for Himself a new people. He has taken out their heart of stone and replaced it with a heart of living flesh. He has recreated them to be a chosen race, a royal priesthood, a holy nation, a people for His own possession; a people who *will* proclaim the excellencies of Him who has called them out of darkness into His marvelous light.[8]

---

6. Matthew 19:26; Mark 10:27; Luke 18:27
7. Genesis 1:2
8. 1 Peter 2:9

This is the great difference between the physical nation of Israel under the old covenant and the true church of Jesus Christ under the new. The nation of Israel was comprised of individuals who shared a common physical ancestry as descendants of Abraham. Nevertheless, the great majority were "mere men" or "natural" men without the Spirit.[9] They remained in the fallen image of their father Adam, were enslaved to the depravity of their hearts, and were driven by the lusts of their flesh.[10] Most did not have the faith of their father Abraham, but were unregenerate, unbelieving, and disobedient. The foundation of the apostle Paul's teaching to the church in Rome was that the majority of those who were descended from Israel were not Israelites at all.[11]

In contrast, the true church under the new covenant is comprised of men and women from every tribe, tongue, people, and nation, and there is no longer any distinction between Greek and Jew, circumcised and uncircumcised, barbarian, Scythian, slave and freeman.[12] Their unity is not in having the same blood as Abraham but in possessing the same faith; they believe God's testimony regarding His Son, and it is reckoned to them as righteousness.[13] They have trusted in Christ as the fulfillment of every promise that God ever made to the patriarchs and the world.[14] Furthermore, the people of the new covenant are united by more than a common calling, religious creed, or shared ethical demands. The Spirit of the living God has regenerated every member of the true church and raised each one up to walk in newness of life.[15] The very God who said, "Light shall shine out of darkness," is the one who has shone in their hearts to give them the light of the knowledge of the glory of God in the

---

9. 1 Corinthians 2:14; 3:3

10. Genesis 5:3; John 8:33–34; Ephesians 2:3

11. Luke 3:7–8; Romans 9:6–8

12. Colossians 3:11; Revelation 5:9

13. Genesis 15:6; Romans 4:3, 16; Galatians 3:6; James 2:23

14. "For all the promises of God in Him are Yes, and in Him Amen, to the glory of God through us" (2 Cor. 1:20). "Now I say that Jesus Christ has become a servant to the circumcision for the truth of God, to confirm the promises made to the fathers, and that the Gentiles might glorify God for His mercy, as it is written: 'For this reason I will confess to You among the Gentiles, and sing to Your name.' And again he says: 'Rejoice, O Gentiles, with His people!' And again: 'Praise the LORD, all you Gentiles! Laud Him, all you peoples!' And again, Isaiah says: 'There shall be a root of Jesse; and He who shall rise to reign over the Gentiles, in Him the Gentiles shall hope'" (Rom. 15:8–12).

15. Romans 6:4

face of Christ.[16] They have been made to see Christ, and they have been transformed so that they might love what they see and be irresistibly bound to Him forever. They are a new people who desire God and delight in His law, not because they come from better stock than the nation of Israel but because the Holy Spirit has recreated them. They have become new creatures in Christ Jesus, the old things have passed away, and new things have come.[17]

ANSWERING ACCUSATIONS AGAINST THE CHURCH

Believers and unbelievers alike often complain that there is just as much wickedness in the church as there is in the unbelieving world. Historians point to the supposed atrocities of the church down through the ages, from the Crusades to the Inquisition. Modern-day pollsters point to statistics that demonstrate the church is filled with sexual immorality, bigotry, greed, hatred, falsehood, and every other vice found in society. Self-proclaimed prophets rail at the church for her supposed abominations and call her everything from Sodom and Gomorra to a wayward prostitute. However, all their accusations are simply not true. They are the result of a singular theological error: they do not have a biblical understanding of the church. Therefore, they accuse the true church for the atrocities committed by those who identify themselves with the church but have no part with her or her Savior.

First, let's look at the supposed atrocities committed by the church in history. One such example is the Holy Inquisition. According to historians, Pope Gregory IX (r. 1227–1241) established the Inquisition, an ecclesiastical tribunal that suppressed heresy, active chiefly in northern Italy and southern France and infamous for its use of torture. In 1542, the Papal Inquisition turned its attention to a new enemy—Protestants. The important truth is that the Inquisition was the tribunal of a singular ecclesiastical organization known as the Roman Catholic Church. How, then, can the true church be blamed for the atrocities of a heretical ecclesiastical organization that persecuted her? A person's confession of faith in Christ is proven false by his misdeeds.[18] The same is true of

---

16. 2 Corinthians 4:6
17. 2 Corinthians 5:17
18. Matthew 7:21–23; James 2:18–19

an ecclesiastical organization's claim to be the true church. As Jesus declared, "A tree is known by its fruit" (Matt. 12:33).

Second, let's look at the statistics of the pollsters who claim that the church is as immoral as the culture that surrounds her. We must recognize that this is an extremely important matter. If the church is as enslaved to vice as the pollsters declare her to be, if she is no better than this godless age, then it throws into question the infallibility of the Scriptures and the integrity of Christianity itself. The Old Testament references to the new covenant clearly promise that God would make for Himself a devout people from Jew and Gentile alike, a people who would reverence Him and walk in obedience. If the church as a whole is no more devout or obedient than the world, then these promises have failed. However, we affirm that neither God nor His Word has failed. The true church of Jesus Christ is faithful, devout, bearing fruit, and growing in conformity to her Lord. Though still struggling against sin and always in need of grace, she stands in stark contrast to the ungodly and immoral culture that surrounds her. The fatal flaw of the pollsters is that they assume that everyone who identifies himself with Christ is Christian and that every organization that calls itself a church is indeed a church.

The pollsters are in error because they have drawn their conclusions from a contaminated field of research. One of the most widely recognized maladies within evangelicalism is that many of those who make a claim to Christianity hold to beliefs and practices that are foreign to biblical and historical Christianity. Even though they may profess some allegiance to Christ, they are not Christian in their doctrine, ethics, or manner of living. Therefore, to assume that they represent the church is absurd, and to draw conclusions about the church based upon their opinions and practices is equally absurd. The following illustrations may be useful in revealing the problem.

It cannot be disputed that the resurrection of Jesus Christ is an essential doctrine. If a person does not fully embrace this doctrine, he cannot be considered Christian by any biblical or historical standard. Therefore, if we poll a thousand individuals who claim to be Christians and discover that 75 percent of them do not believe in the resurrection, we cannot logically conclude that 75 percent of all Christians do not believe in the resurrection. Rather, a more logical conclusion would be that 75 percent of the individuals who believe they are Christians are not Christians at all. To further the argument, let's say that there is a neighborhood church that is infamous for its hatred, strife, and bickering. During a monthly business meeting, a terrible argument breaks out that pits half the church against the other half. The meeting is filled with wrath, dissension, name-calling, and vicious threats. Finally, one godly man in the congregation stands up and shouts, "We are Christians, and therefore we should not hate one another." However, he would have been more correct if he said, "We hate one another, and, therefore, we are not Christians!"[19]

The true church is not as immoral and godless as the culture that surrounds it. Though not yet glorified, the true church is marked by holiness, devotion, and obedience. When she does stumble and fall into sin, she is broken, repentant, and willing to acknowledge her sin before God and man. Those who believe otherwise have little understanding of the true nature of the church or the greatness of the new covenant promises upon which she is established.

Third, let's consider the well-meaning "prophets" who rail at the church for her supposed abominations and call her everything from Sodom and Gomorra to a wayward prostitute. When we look at what people presently call the church, we do see many abominations and harlotries. Often a type of immorality exists within the so-called church that does not exist even among unbelievers; there are disgraceful things of which we cannot even speak without contaminating ourselves.[20] However, these things are not the common practice of the true bride of Christ but are the deeds of wolves in sheep's clothing and of tares that grow together with the wheat.[21]

The true church is not immune to sin and can become entangled for a time in worldly affairs. Likewise, the true believer will struggle against sin and may even fall grievously. However, neither the true church nor the true believer lives a life marked by the godlessness and immoralities of this age. A rose by any other name is still a rose because it bears the characteristics of a rose regardless of the name it is given. However, a thistle is still a thistle, even if it is called a rose. We must make a distinction between those who publicly identify themselves with Christ and His church, and those who truly are Christians and members of Christ's body.

---

19. This illustration comes from Pastor Charles Leiter of Lake Road Chapel in Kirksville, Missouri.

20. 1 Corinthians 5:1; Ephesians 5:12

21. Matthew 7:15; 13:24–30, 36–43

Based upon this truth, the "prophets" who rail against the church should use caution in their evaluation and in the manner by which they address her. We should not blame the sheep for the deeds of goats, nor should we burn down the wheat field because of the tares. Furthermore, is it not a fearful thing to address the bride of Christ as Sodom and Gomorra or to insult her as a prostitute? It is true that such language is used in the Old Testament with regard to the nation of Israel, but we must remember that God was primarily addressing an unregenerate people whose hearts were made of hostile stone and whose deeds were often worse than those of the pagans around them. However, no one should use such hard language against the true church, the bride of Christ. No respectable man would stand idly by while another railed accusations of infidelity, uncleanness, and whoredom against his wife. Do we think that Christ would tolerate such treatment of His dear bride? Though we must tell her of her sin, we must never forget whom we are addressing and to whom she belongs.

For this reason, the New Testament prophets are told to speak to the church for "edification and exhortation and comfort" (1 Cor. 14:3). They are not instructed to rail at her for crimes she has not committed or to insult her with words unfit for the coarsest and most unrefined among us. We should be jealous for the church with a "godly jealousy," but our esteem for her position as the bride of Christ ought to temper the fire in our tongues (2 Cor. 11:2). We should do all within our power to present the church to Christ as a pure virgin.[22] However, we must take care never to overpower her or treat her roughly.

THE APPARENT CARNALITY OF THE CHURCH EXPLAINED

At this point, we must ask a few important questions. Why does the true church seem to be so indiscernible in the world, and why are there so many who identify themselves with Christ and yet bear little of His fruit? Why do carnal people seem to be the majority in the contemporary evangelical church, while the spiritual and devout appear to be a tiny remnant? Although we might fill an entire book with explanations, we must confine ourselves to only a few.

First, the vast number of carnal people who identify themselves with the church is the result of the unbiblical gospel preached from

---

22. 2 Corinthians 11:2

most evangelical pulpits. As has been stated throughout this book, we have taken the gospel of Jesus Christ and reduced it to a few creedal statements that a person is called to accept. We have removed its radical demands and most of its scandal. We downplay the supremacy and worth of God above His creation, and we place man on center stage in the divine theater. We rarely mention the radical depravity of man and the heinous nature of his sin or expound it to wound the conscience. We have replaced the call to repentance and faith with the repetition of a prayer. Ecclesiastical authorities grant assurance of salvation with little concern for the evidences of conversion. The costly call of radical discipleship and the demand for holiness are all but absent. For these reasons, the carnal and the unconverted can make a claim to Zion and dwell inside her walls with no affliction of conscience or contradiction of mind.

Second, the vast number of carnal people who identify with the church comes from our low view of conversion. The understanding of regeneration has nearly been lost, and the term *born again* has come to mean "making a decision for Christ" and "praying the sinner's prayer." Furthermore, many believe that a person can be truly born again and yet live his entire life in worldliness. The church not only tolerates continuous carnality in the church, but it also seems to expect it. The radical nature of regeneration as a supernatural recreating work of the Holy Spirit seems beyond our grasp. People no longer seem to believe in the gospel's power to subdue sin in the life of a convert and compel him to greater Christlikeness. Preachers rarely proclaim the apostolic message that demanded that people "should repent, turn to God, and do works befitting repentance" (Acts 26:20). The admonition to "make [our] calling and election sure" is as absent from our preaching as power is from our pulpits (2 Peter 1:10). We no longer think the need to examine and test ourselves to see if we are in the faith is necessary.[23] Thus, the carnal sing the songs of Zion, thinking they have heaven as a future home, even though this world has their present heart.

Before the Great Awakening, refined but carnal people filled the churches. They felt assured of their place before God because of their baptism, confirmation, or civility. They thought themselves to be thoroughly Christian in a thoroughly Christian nation. However, God raised up the likes of George Whitefield, John and Charles Wesley, Howell Harris,

---

23. 2 Corinthians 13:5

and Daniel Rowland, whose message rocked England and Wales to the core. The strength of their message was founded upon their belief that the gospel was the power of God not only to deliver a person from the condemnation of sin, but also from its dominion. They preached regeneration as a miraculous event that could change the vilest sinner into a saint of the living God. When these men's preaching confronted them, the carnal congregants in the church lost their false assurance and either ran to Calvary or became infuriated and attacked those who would dare question the sincerity of their faith or the validity of their conversion.

The same must occur today if we are ever to see revival and reformation. In Whitefield's day, carnal people found assurance in their baptism and confirmation. In our day, the same kind of carnal people find their assurance in the apparent sincerity of a decision they once made and a prayer they once prayed. Well-meaning pastors who welcome them into the family of God without discernment, proper instruction, or the necessary gospel warnings confirm their false assurance. If we long for reformation and revival in what we know as the evangelical church, then the cry from the pulpit must be, "You must be born again." Yet before we can properly proclaim this truth, we must first understand what it means.

Third, many carnal people identify themselves with the church because the church communicates a wrong message of its relevancy to the world. The erroneous, but prevailing theory of the day is that church must look as much like the world as possible in order to be relevant and reach people for Christ. Thus, we change our look, our services, and our focus. We become interested in things that interest carnal people so that they will become interested in us. This is a grave error. The church is not relevant to the world because we look and act like the world or share its interests. We are relevant because we seek to submit ourselves to Christ in every aspect of life, and He transforms our interests, actions, and appearance. It is our distinction from the world that makes us relevant, and the greater our distinction, the greater our relevancy. The distinctiveness of salt causes it to impact the thing upon which it is poured. The unique qualities of light distinguish it from darkness.

People will not come to Christ because we have converted the church into a vanity fair, sporting arena, or entertainment center. If we use carnal means to attract carnal people, we must continue to use carnal means to keep them. We will not be able, as some suppose, to change the menu to a more spiritual diet halfway through the meal. Apart from a supernatural work of the Spirit through a right preaching of the gospel, people will never have a palate for the Bread that came down from heaven.[24]

Furthermore, in our constant catering to carnal people, we are allowing the true sheep to starve to death. They do not want entertainment. They desire worship. They cannot live on quaint antidotes, moral stories, or life principles. They need the true milk and meat of God's Word.[25] They could care less about their felt needs. They want to learn obedience and service to God. They do not want their ear tickled or their self-esteem coddled. They want to be conformed to the image of Christ. They do not need what they are fed in most seeker friendly, culturally relevant sideshows. They just want to know God and Jesus Christ, whom He has sent.[26] In addition, what a terror it will be for the pastor, elder, or teacher who has spent his life and ministry wooing the worldly and catering to the passions of the carnal while allowing Christ's sheep to go unfed and uncared for.

Fourth, the number of carnal people who identify themselves with the church is the result of our failure to obey God in the matter of church discipline. Though church discipline is an undeniable aspect of church life in the New Testament, it is widely misunderstood among evangelicals.[27] The most common argument used against church discipline is that it is unloving and judgmental. In rebuttal, we merely need to point to the teachings of our Lord, who commanded such a practice. If we are unloving in obeying the command, was He unloving in giving it? Although we are not to judge with critical and censorious attitudes, we are commanded to judge and even expel if necessary.[28] If in the consummation of all things we are going to judge angels, are we not now able to judge matters pertaining to the church and her well-being?[29]

Our boasting in a love that refuses to confront unrepentant sin is not good. Do we not understand that a little leaven leavens the whole lump of dough?[30] Are we demonstrating love toward God when we allow sin

---

24. John 6:26, 35
25. Hebrews 5:14; 1 Peter 2:2
26. John 17:3
27. Matthew 18:15–20; 1 Corinthians 5:1–5; 2 Thessalonians 3:6, 14
28. Matthew 7:1–5, 15–20; 1 Corinthians 5:13
29. 1 Corinthians 6:3
30. 1 Corinthians 5:6

to run rampant in the church so that God's name is blasphemed among unbelievers?[31] Are we demonstrating love toward our brothers in Christ when we allow them to be destroyed by habitual sin, or are we demonstrating self-love and refusing to enter into conflict for the sake of self-preservation?

CONCLUSION

We would do well to remember that the church belongs to God, and it is Christ's bride. We have no authority to do what seems right in our own eyes. We must submit to the lordship of Christ and care for the church in accordance with His Word. We must minister to God's people in God's way.

How little of the true gospel is preached in our day! How many people sit at ease in pews even though they are not saved? How many so-called churches serve to please carnal-minded people while God's lambs languish, starving for the Word, true worship, and godly fellowship? How often is the name of God blasphemed among unbelievers whose opinions of Christ and the church have been eroded by the testimony of carnal people who claim Christ and yet have no part with Him?

We must return to a biblical understanding of conversion as a supernatural work of the Holy Spirit that will result in ongoing sanctification and fruit bearing. We must return to a biblical understanding of the true church as a redeemed community of spiritual men and women who have come to know Christ and desire nothing more and nothing less. We must put away the practice of making the church look like a vanity fair in an attempt to impress carnal people and draw their interest. God has ordained to create for Himself a people that will claim Him as their God. He has ordained to do it through the proclamation of His glorious gospel and the testimony of His saints as they walk in simplicity, holiness, and love, proving themselves to be blameless children of God above reproach in the midst of a crooked and perverse generation, among whom they appear as lights in the world.[32]

---

31. Romans 2:24
32. Philippians 2:15

CHAPTER THIRTEEN

The Christian's Sure Knowledge of God

No more shall every man teach his neighbor, and every man his brother, saying, "Know the LORD," for they all shall know Me, from the least of them to the greatest of them, says the LORD. For I will forgive their iniquity, and their sin I will remember no more.
　　　　　　　　　　　　　　　　　　　　　　　　　　　—Jeremiah 31:34

Here we have a most amazing prophecy that every member of the church will possess a real, intimate knowledge of God. We should not understand this as metaphor or hyperbole but as an Old Testament prophecy that is fulfilled in the New Testament Christian. The writer of Hebrews confirms this truth, quoting the text at length and applying it to the church of Jesus Christ: "None of them shall teach his neighbor, and none his brother, saying, 'Know the LORD,' for all shall know Me, from the least of them to the greatest of them. For I will be merciful to their unrighteousness, and their sins and their lawless deeds I will remember no more" (8:11–12).

IGNORANCE UNDER THE OLD COVENANT

To comprehend the significance of this promise, we must first understand its context. Under the old covenant, the knowledge of God seemed confined to a relatively small group of individuals. Prophets, priests, scribes, and sometimes kings were among its common recipients. In turn, they were responsible for their knowledge and were obliged to instruct the rest of the covenant community of Israel. However, such instruction appears to have been a rather daunting task, not only because of the sheer number of Israelites but also because of Israel's spiritual blindness and hardness of heart. In fact, this self-imposed ignorance seems to have been the cause for one of God's greatest and most frequent accusations against His old covenant people.

> Hear the word of the LORD,
> You children of Israel,
> For the LORD brings a charge against the inhabitants
>   of the land:
> "There is no truth or mercy
> Or knowledge of God in the land" (Hos. 4:1).

> For My people are foolish,
> They have not known Me.
> They are silly children,
> And they have no understanding.
> They are wise to do evil,
> But to do good they have no knowledge (Jer. 4:22).

> That this is a rebellious people,
> Lying children,
> Children who will not hear the law of the LORD;
> Who say to the seers, "Do not see,"
> And to the prophets, "Do not prophesy to us right
>   things;
> Speak to us smooth things, prophesy deceits.
> Get out of the way,
> Turn aside from the path,
> Cause the Holy One of Israel
> To cease from before us" (Isa. 30:9–11).

From these texts, we understand why God often warned His prophets that He was sending them to a people who would not listen. He told Isaiah that he was to go to a people whose hearts were insensitive, whose ears were dull, and whose eyes were dim.[1] He warned Jeremiah that he must speak to a foolish people who had no knowledge of God and to stupid children who had no understanding.[2] Finally, in His commissioning of Ezekiel as a prophet to Israel, God declared, "Surely, had I sent you to them, they would have listened to you. But the house of Israel will not listen to you, because they will not listen to Me; for all the house of Israel are impudent and hard-hearted. Behold, I have made your face strong

---

1. Isaiah 6:10
2. Jeremiah 4:22; 10:14

against their faces, and your forehead strong against their foreheads" (Ezek. 3:6–8).

By the time of the prophets, Israel had demonstrated its willful ignorance of God. However, their lack of knowledge was not the result of a hiding God, but rather the people's hardened hearts, their love for sin, and their desire to "cause the Holy One of Israel to cease from before us" (Isa. 30:11). In almost every case, Israel's ignorance of the one true God is attributed to the depraved condition of its heart. The prophet Jeremiah accredited the people's lack of knowledge to their foolishness and intimate acquaintance with evil.[3] Isaiah blames their hardened hearts and rebellious attitudes toward God.[4] Ezekiel points his indicting finger to their stubbornness and obstinacy.[5]

The apostle Paul clearly sets forth in the New Testament this direct relationship between the people's ignorance of God and the depravity of the human heart, attributing all of humankind's ignorance to the "ungodliness and unrighteousness of men, who suppress the truth in unrighteousness."[6] This is why ignorance is considered a crime and the ignorant are treated as criminals. It is for this reason God finally exiled the Israelites for a lack of understanding and destroyed them for a lack of knowledge.[7]

THE PROMISE OF THE KNOWLEDGE OF GOD

In the new covenant prophecies of the Old Testament, God promised to make a people for Himself that would know Him, fear Him, and walk in His commandments. Furthermore, He promised to accomplish such a goal through the coming of the Messiah: His incarnation, atonement, and power to raise the spiritually dead to life.[8]

According to the Old Testament Scriptures, one of the primary results of the Messiah's coming would be that He would deliver His people from their spiritual blindness and subsequent moral bondage. The messianic

---

3. Jeremiah 4:22

4. Isaiah 6:10; 30:9

5. Ezekiel 3:7

6. Romans 1:18

7. Isaiah 5:13; Hosea 4:6

8. "Most assuredly, I say to you, the hour is coming, and now is, when the dead will hear the voice of the Son of God; and those who hear will live" (John 5:25).

prophecy from Isaiah 42:6–7 clearly reveals this truth. In this text, God both commissions the Messiah and explains the purpose of His work:

> I, the LORD, have called You in righteousness,
> And will hold Your hand;
> I will keep You and give You as a covenant to the people,
> As a light to the Gentiles,
> To open blind eyes,
> To bring out prisoners from the prison,
> Those who sit in darkness from the prison house.

As the incarnate Son of God, the Messiah would not merely be a bearer of the light, but He would be the light itself. He would not be one revelation among many others, but He would be the greatest revelation of God that the world would ever know. For this reason, the prophet Isaiah declared that the people who walked in darkness would see a great light, and upon those in a dark land, the light would shine.[9] The prophet Habakkuk added to Isaiah's announcement by declaring that the revelation of God through the Messiah would not be confined to a mere region or to one people, but through Him the entire earth would be filled with the knowledge of the glory of the Lord, as the waters cover the sea.[10] Consequently, this knowledge would produce such devotion among the people that from the rising of the sun even to its setting, God's name would be great among the nations.[11]

Through the incarnation, the knowledge of God would shine into the darkest places of this fallen world. However, given what the Scriptures teach us regarding the depravity of the human heart and its hostility toward the knowledge of God, we understand that the greatest of revelations will have little effect upon the human heart unless it is somehow transformed to receive it. Before the knowledge of God can flourish in the individual or the collective community, the heart must be renewed or transformed. It is for this reason that the new covenant promises of the Old Testament not only look forward to the Messiah's revelation of God but also to His power to resurrect the human heart and make it a willing recipient of that revelation. As God declared through the prophet Jeremiah, "I will give them a heart to know Me" (Jer. 24:7).

---

9. Isaiah 9:2; Matthew 4:15–16
10. Isaiah 11:9; Habakkuk 2:14
11. Malachi 1:11

This promise stands at the core of the new covenant. God would take out His people's hearts of stone and replace them with hearts of flesh.[12] He would then write His law upon their new hearts, and they would all know Him—from the least of them to the greatest of them.[13] Thus, He would remove the darkness that surrounded His people, and every living member of His covenant community would have a real, intimate knowledge of His person and will, from the most uneducated in the most primitive tribe to the greatest scholars and churchmen of history. The prophet Hosea beautifully summarizes the entire matter:

> I will betroth you to Me forever;
> Yes, I will betroth you to Me
> In righteousness and justice,
> In lovingkindness and mercy;
> I will betroth you to Me in faithfulness,
> And you shall know the Lord (2:19–20).

THE PROMISE FULFILLED

What was only promised and longed for in the prophecies of the Old Testament is wonderfully fulfilled in the New Testament through the person and work of Jesus Christ. The writers of the New Testament claim that Jesus of Nazareth is the true light of which the prophets spoke. Coming into the world, He enlightens every man.[14] He is the Light of the World, and the one who follows Him "shall not walk in darkness, but have the light of life" (John 8:12). No one has seen God at any time, but He who is always at the Father's side has explained Him.[15] The one who has seen the Son has seen the Father, for the Son is the image of the invisible God, the radiance of His glory, and the exact representation of His nature.[16]

The Old Testament prophecies looked forward to a superior sacrifice that would remove the iniquity of the land in one day.[17] This sacrifice would open up a fountain for the house of David for cleansing of sin and

---

12. Ezekiel 36:26
13. Jeremiah 31:33–34
14. John 1:9
15. John 1:18
16. John 14:9; Colossians 1:15; Hebrews 1:1–3
17. Zechariah 3:9

impurity.[18] It would enable a just God to forgive His people's iniquity and remember their sin no more.[19] It would have the power to betroth God's people to Him forever in righteousness and justice.[20] The writers of the New Testament claim that Jesus of Nazareth is this once-for-all sacrifice.[21] He is the Lamb of God who takes away the sin of the world.[22] His blood was the blood of the new covenant, which was poured out for many for forgiveness of sins.[23] He has become for His people wisdom, righteousness, sanctification, and redemption.[24] Through Him, they have now received the reconciliation.[25] He Himself is their peace.[26]

The Old Testament prophecies looked forward to a time when all of God's people, from the greatest of them to the least of them, would know Him—a time when the earth would be full of the knowledge of God as the waters cover the sea.[27] The writers of the New Testament claim that Jesus Christ ushered in such an age through His death, resurrection, and outpouring of the Holy Spirit.[28] Through His regenerating work, a person's heart is transformed from a hardened path that rejects the gospel seed into a heart of good soil that humbly receives the Word implanted.[29] This rejuvenated and fertile heart is "taught of God" to esteem Christ and draw near to Him for salvation (John 6:45). Such an impartation of knowledge is not natural; rather, it is a miraculous work of the Holy Spirit, and it is comparable to the first day of creation, when God called forth light out of the midst of primeval darkness. The apostle Paul describes it in this way: "For it is the God who commanded light to shine out of darkness, who has shone in our hearts to give the light of the knowledge of the glory of God in the face of Jesus Christ" (2 Cor. 4:6).

We simply cannot exaggerate the extraordinary and supernatural nature of God's work in every true believer's heart and mind. This

---

18. Zechariah 13:1
19. Jeremiah 31:34
20. Hosea 2:19–20
21. Hebrews 7:27; 9:12; 10:10
22. John 1:29
23. Matthew 26:28
24. 1 Corinthians 1:30
25. Romans 5:11
26. Ephesians 2:14
27. Isaiah 11:9; Jeremiah 31:34; Habakkuk 2:14
28. Acts 2:16–21
29. Matthew 13:19; James 1:21

illuminating work of Christ through the Holy Spirit in the heart of the Christian is a mark of true conversion and is promised to all without exception. For this reason, the apostle John did not hesitate to write the following declaration regarding every true believer: "And we know that the Son of God has come and has given us an understanding, that we may know Him who is true; and we are in Him who is true, in His Son Jesus Christ. This is the true God and eternal life" (1 John 5:20).

This sure knowledge of God that will be a reality in the life of every believer is the result of the regenerating work of the Holy Spirit. Because of His ongoing ministry of illumination and sanctification, the darkness is passing away, and the true light is already shining in every child of God.[30] In the same letter, the beloved apostle assured even the youngest converts that they had been anointed by the Spirit and knew the truth about God.[31] He went so far as to say that this anointing was so powerful that they had no need for anyone to teach them, for the Spirit of God was teaching them about all things necessary for life and godliness.[32]

This does not mean that Christians have no need of godly teachers. The Scriptures are clear that God has given gifted teachers to the church to equip the saints and build up the body of Christ.[33] Instead, it means that the believer (unlike unregenerate Israelites under the old covenant) is no longer solely dependent upon a human mediator to dictate to him the truth of God. All true believers have been "taught by God" to embrace His Son and "taught by God to love one another" (John 6:45; 1 Thess. 4:9). God's teaching ministry will continue throughout the believer's life, and God's acts of providence, the Scriptures, and the Holy Spirit, who gives understanding, will accomplish it. In response, the Christian is to work out his salvation in fear and trembling, to press on to know the Lord, and to be diligent to present himself approved to God as a workman who does not need to be ashamed, accurately handling the word of truth.[34] In the words of the apostle Peter, the believer is to "grow in the grace

---

30. 1 John 2:8

31. "But you have an anointing from the Holy One, and you know all things" (1 John 2:20). The anointing that all believers receive is probably a reference to the work of regeneration and the indwelling of the Spirit of God in the heart of the believer.

32. 1 John 2:27

33. Ephesians 4:11–12

34. Hosea 6:2–3; Philippians 2:12; 2 Timothy 2:15

and knowledge of [his] Lord and Savior Jesus Christ" and to bear fruit in accordance with that knowledge.[35]

A PRACTICAL APPLICATION

Through the atoning work of Christ and the regenerating work of the Holy Spirit, God has made for Himself a new people. He has reconciled them and transformed them into a collective group of individuals who both know Him and desire to know Him more. They are a people who have come to understand something of the great realities that ought to govern their lives, such as who God is, what they were, what God has done for them, and how they should live before Him. God has given them eternal life that they may know the only true God and Jesus Christ, whom He has sent.[36] God has told them what is good and what He requires of them: to do justice, to love kindness, and to walk humbly with their God.[37] This real, personal knowledge of God and His will is a distinguishing mark of the true church and will be an ongoing reality in the life of every true believer. As Jesus said to the hostile Jewish leaders who opposed Him: "My sheep hear My voice, and I know them, and they follow Me" (John 10:27).

We often hear that God refers to His people as sheep because sheep are rather stupid creatures that are prone to wandering. However, in light of Christ's description of His sheep, this idea seems to be a contradiction of the teaching of Scripture. Christ calls His people sheep because they, unlike the roguish and obstinate goats, clearly discern His voice and meekly follow Him. What, then, is the basis for this popular and harmful cliché? It is an erroneous reverse logic. Instead of looking to the Scriptures for a biblical description of the individual sheep or the collective flock, most form their opinions by observing the characteristics of those who identify themselves with evangelical Christianity. Since many professing Christians in the West are ignorant of the rudimentary truths of God and seem deaf to the voice of the Master, we assume that God's sheep are little more than dumb-witted animals who are constantly wandering and unable to discern their Master's voice. We forget that Christ says that His sheep hear His voice, and they follow Him. Therefore, it is

---

35. 2 Peter 1:8; 3:18
36. John 17:3
37. Micah 6:8

more biblical to suppose that many of those who profess Christ within the evangelical community are not true sheep. Instead, they are unregenerate goats who live as they do because of what they are. On that final day, Christ will set them to the left of the flock, and they will hear the terrifying verdict from Christ Himself: "Depart from Me, you cursed, into the everlasting fire prepared for the devil and his angels."[38]

One of the distinguishing characteristics of the true Christian individually and the invisible church collectively is their knowledge of God and their response to it. Although all Christians stand in need of discipleship, and the work of sanctification is never fully accomplished in this life, there will be a notable difference in the true Christian's knowledge of God and his submission to that knowledge. This difference will be evident even in the life of the most recent convert. By virtue of his regenerated heart and the indwelling Spirit, he will possess a certain, definite knowledge of who God is and what His law requires. He will recognize the wrongness of sin and the rightness of obedience. No one will have to tell him not to lie, steal, commit adultery, or take the name of his Savior lightly. He will possess knowledge of these things and increase in it because the God who began a good work in him will continue to perfect it.[39]

In conclusion, we must ask ourselves these questions: Is there any evidence that we have been "taught of God," or are we ignorant of the rudimentary truths of our faith? Are we growing in our knowledge, or are we unmoved in our apathy? Are we increasingly governed by what we know, or is there little evidence of progress in godliness? Do we hear the Master's voice and follow Him, or are we deaf and blind rogues who choose our own way? Do we have the sure knowledge that God has forgiven our sin and forgotten our iniquities for the sake of His Son, who died and rose again on our behalf? The professing Christian must answer these questions, and it is the duty of the faithful minister of Christ to impress these questions upon the heart and conscience of his flock.

---

38. Matthew 25:31–33, 41
39. Philippians 1:6

CHAPTER FOURTEEN

The Heart and Way
of God's People

They shall be My people, and I will be their God; then I will give them one heart and one way, that they may fear Me forever, for the good of them and their children after them.

—Jeremiah 32:38–39

Before us is one of the most beautiful of all the new covenant promises in the Old Testament. It is an eloquent, yet powerful declaration of God's sovereignty: He has decreed to make for Himself a people, and He will do it. Although this work of redemption will span the full course of human history, our confidence should not waiver. What divine sovereignty has decreed, divine power will accomplish. As God declared through the prophet Isaiah:

> For as the rain comes down, and the snow from heaven,
> And do not return there,
> But water the earth,
> And make it bring forth and bud,
> That it may give seed to the sower
> And bread to the eater,
> So shall My word be that goes forth from My mouth;
> It shall not return to Me void,
> But it shall accomplish what I please,
> And it shall prosper in the thing for which I sent it
> (55:10–11).

In accordance with God's decree, when the fullness of time came, He sent forth His Son, born of a woman, born under the law, to redeem a people for Himself.[1] For the last two thousand years, He has applied this

---

1. Galatians 4:4

work of redemption to a countless multitude through the preaching of the gospel and the regenerating work of the Holy Spirit. By these means He has made for Himself a true church, of which it may be said, "They are His people, and He is their God." By His sovereign grace, He has separated them from the rest of humanity and made them His treasured possession.[2] By this same grace, He has turned their affections Godward, so that nothing they desire compares with Him.[3] They have tasted and seen that the Lord is good.[4] They have discovered for themselves that in His presence is fullness of joy and in His right hand are pleasures forever.[5] Accordingly, they esteem one day in His courts to be better than a thousand elsewhere, and they would rather stand at the threshold of the house of their God than dwell in the opulent tents of the secular man.[6] He is their God, and they are His people. He has given them one heart, one way, and one fear for their own good and the good of countless generations after them.

ONE HEART

After declaring His unwavering commitment to create a people for Himself, God reveals the first characteristic of that people: they would have one heart. They would be united in their affections for God, in their love for each other, and in the purpose and conduct of their lives. In other words, they would be one.[7]

For many sincere believers this promise seems to present a great problem. In light of the numerous denominations within Christianity and the almost endless variety of doctrinal deviations, how can we affirm that the new covenant promise of unity has been fulfilled in the church? The answer to this apparent problem is twofold. First, we must

---

2. Deuteronomy 26:18
3. Proverbs 3:14–15
4. Psalm 34:8
5. Psalm 16:11
6. Psalm 84:10
7. "And other sheep I have which are not of this fold; them also I must bring, and they will hear My voice; and there will be one flock and one shepherd" (John 10:16). "Now I am no longer in the world, but these are in the world, and I come to You. Holy Father, keep through Your name those whom You have given Me, that they may be one as We are" (John 17:11). "That they all may be one, as You, Father, are in Me, and I in You; that they also may be one in Us, that the world may believe that You sent Me" (John 17:21).

recognize that whenever genuine, Spirit-filled Christians come together there will be a bond of unity and love between them that will far outweigh the total of all their peripheral doctrinal differences. Second, we must realize that much of the so-called division in Christianity is the result of the often forgotten truth that not every person who professes Christ is truly Christian, and not every religious organization that calls itself a church is truly a church.

REAL UNITY

As Christians, we recognize the importance of truth and the dangers of deviating from it. For this reason, we are passionate about what we believe, quick to defend it, and tenacious in publicizing our beliefs to others. When we add to this mix the real possibility that we may be guilty of pride, self-centeredness, selfishness, and the desire to be vindicated in all that we say and do, it is easy to see how relationships with our brothers and sisters in Christ can become difficult. In fact, it is a testimony to the supernatural nature of conversion that such passionate individuals can exist together at all.

The New Testament gives testimony that the church is not immune to division.[8] Even the apostle Paul and the beloved Barnabas separated from one another for a time.[9] In spite of this, it is undeniable that whenever genuine, Spirit-filled Christians come together, there will be a bond of unity and love between them that will go beyond anything that the world can conjure. Their love for God and His dear Son, their appreciation of Calvary, their comprehension of grace, and the indwelling Spirit will unite them. It will lead them to bear one another's burdens, minister to each other's needs, and even lay down their lives for one another if necessary. This is not empty rhetoric. It has been the testimony of true Christians everywhere throughout the history of the church. Love for the brethren has always been the distinguishing mark of genuine Christianity.[10]

Imagine the following scenario: A young American missionary is visiting churches in the high jungles of South America. Terrorists patrol the area, and the journey is dangerous. One night, the missionary loses his way and comes upon a small village. He knows that it is unwise to

---

8. 1 Corinthians 1:10–12; 11:18; Philippians 4:2
9. Acts 15:37–40
10. John 13:35; 1 John 2:9–11; 4:7–12

stay the night in the jungle, and yet he hesitates to enter the village for fear that it might be sympathetic to the terrorists. Finally, fear gives way to necessity, and he knocks on the door of a small adobe hut carved into the side of the hill. In a few minutes, a tiny old woman holding a lantern opens the door. She is obviously frightened and asks for the visitor's name. When he replies that he is a Christian missionary, she takes him by the coat and draws him inside. She warns him that it is not safe and then hides him in the dugout basement of her home. As he rests upon a pile of corn stalks, the old woman tells a young boy to call together the brothers of the church and instruct them to bring food. Within the hour, believers arrive with a freshly killed chicken and several potatoes that they quickly cook up and serve to the hungry missionary. As they talk during the meal, the hosts discover that their guest is a Baptist, and he discovers that they are Nazarenes. There is much about which they differ, but that night, all of it seems inconsequential. They are a tiny body of believers, loving one another as though they were flesh and blood and caring for one another's needs as though each thought the other to be Christ Himself. The missionary had placed himself in danger to bring them the Scriptures, and they had done the same to harbor him for a night. Despite their doctrinal differences, they showed themselves to be of one heart just as Jeremiah had prophesied.[11]

In His High Priestly Prayer the night before His crucifixion, the Lord Jesus Christ petitioned the Father that His people might be one.[12] We must not think that the Father has faltered in answering this prayer or that one jot or tittle of this new covenant promise has failed. Whenever genuine believers come together in the name of Christ, there may be differences, discrepancies, and even disagreements, but there will always be love. If there is not, then their very profession of faith should be called into question.

NECESSARY DIVISIONS

Many individuals and movements within Western evangelicalism identify themselves with Christ, yet they stand outside the current of historic Christianity. Their doctrines and practices are so contrary to the rule

---

11. Jeremiah 32:38–39
12. John 17:11

of Scripture that they cannot logically be identified with the Christian faith. Either they are right and all of historic Christianity is wrong, or they are the false teachers and false brethren about which Christ and the apostles warned us: "But there were also false prophets among the people, even as there will be false teachers among you, who will secretly bring in destructive heresies, even denying the Lord who bought them, and bring on themselves swift destruction. And many will follow their destructive ways, because of whom the way of truth will be blasphemed" (2 Peter 2:1–2).

Although divisions do occur between sincere Christians, it is important to realize that the supposed great and frequent divisions within the whole of Christianity are not so much between the members of Christ's body, but between the wheat and the tares, the sheep and the goats, the good shepherds and the wolves.[13] For this reason, the apostle Paul wrote to the church in Corinth that there must be some factions or divisions among those who identify themselves with Christ in order that those who are approved of God may become evident.[14] In other words, God has a twofold purpose for division: first, to reveal those who are genuinely Christian and to expose those who are not; and second, to remove the false teachers and false brethren from the body so that they might not further defile His people.

Within evangelicalism are many popular teachers who have gained great followings. Their meetings fill huge stadiums, and they broadcast services around the world. Their teachings are a mixture of ancient heresy, modern psychology, humanism, and sensuality. They promote self-realization, material prosperity, physical health, and temporal joys. As a result, many are drawn away from historic Christianity, and, like Hymenaeus and Alexander, they make a shipwreck of their faith.[15] Such a thing is heartbreaking and difficult to bear, and yet we must be careful to recognize that God is at work in the matter. He is using these false teachers to draw away the goats from the sheep and place them in a separate corral in order to protect His fold from their doctrinal and ethical errors. As an ancient doctor might prepare a poultice to draw the venom from a wound, God uses these false prophets to draw out the unbelieving

13. Matthew 13:24–30, 36–43; 25:31–33; 7:15; Acts 20:29–30
14. 1 Corinthians 11:19
15. 1 Timothy 1:19–20

and unregenerate from among His people so that their poison might not spring up and defile many.[16]

When the church as a whole is neglectful of Christ's command to practice church discipline, He takes the matter into His own hands.[17] Like a good shepherd, He sees to it that no immoral or godless person like Esau remains long among His people.[18] If a church is really a church and Christ is really among them, then He will be like a refiner's fire and a fuller's soap. He will sit as a smelter and purifier of silver and will refine His people like gold.[19] However, if the godless remain in the congregation without Christ's intervention, it is evidence that their candlestick has been removed and the church is no longer a church. Ichabod has been written over the door, for the glory of the Lord has departed.[20]

ONE WAY

Under the old covenant, the nation of Israel was marked by roguishness. It was like a horse or mule that has no understanding and requires a bit and bridle to hold it in check.[21] For this reason, God declared through the prophet Isaiah, "I have stretched out My hands all day long to a rebellious people, who walk in a way that is not good, according to their own thoughts" (30:8). Repeatedly, God called out to Israel:

> Stand in the ways and see,
> And ask for the old paths, where the good way is,
> And walk in it;
> Then you will find rest for your souls.
> But [Israel] said, "We will not walk in it" (Jer. 6:16).

Like sheep who had gone astray, each had turned to His own way.[22]

In the midst of Israel's rebellion, God sent His prophets, not only to rebuke and warn the nation but also to prophesy of a day when He would create a new people for Himself who would both listen and obey. They would have no need of bits and bridles or tutors, for the Holy Spirit

---

16. Hebrews 12:15
17. Matthew 18:15–18
18. Hebrews 12:15–16
19. Malachi 3:2–3
20. 1 Samuel 4:21
21. Psalm 32:9
22. Isaiah 53:6

would transform, indwell, and lead them.[23] God would give them a new heart that would hunger and thirst after righteousness, and His providence would guide them in paths of righteousness for His name's sake.[24] They would have a common purpose and ethic. They would walk in the way marked out for them by the Messiah. It would be a way of holiness, righteousness, and love. The prophet Isaiah beautifully and powerfully illustrates this truth:

> A highway shall be there, and a road,
> And it shall be called the Highway of Holiness.
> The unclean shall not pass over it,
> But it shall be for others.
> Whoever walks the road, although a fool,
> Shall not go astray.
> No lion shall be there,
> Nor shall any ravenous beast go up on it;
> It shall not be found there.
> But the redeemed shall walk there (35:8–9).

> Yet your teachers will not be moved into a corner anymore,
> But your eyes shall see your teachers.
> Your ears shall hear a word behind you, saying,
> "This is the way, walk in it,"
> Whenever you turn to the right hand
> Or whenever you turn to the left (30:20–21).

> I will bring the blind by a way they did not know;
> I will lead them in paths they have not known.
> I will make darkness light before them,
> And crooked places straight.
> These things I will do for them,
> And not forsake them (42:16).

In the new covenant promises of the Old Testament, God looked forward to a time when He would not only create a new people, but He would also set them on a new course, and He would watch over them to ensure they would not depart from it. Ezekiel prophesied that God

---

23. "But before faith came, we were kept under guard by the law, kept for the faith which would afterward be revealed. Therefore the law was our tutor to bring us to Christ, that we might be justified by faith. But after faith has come, we are no longer under a tutor. For you are all sons of God through faith in Christ Jesus" (Gal. 3:23–26).

24. Psalm 23:3; Matthew 5:6

would give His people a new heart, put His Spirit within them, and cause them to walk in the way of His statutes.[25] Jeremiah foretold of a day when God would give His people one way and teach them to walk in it.[26] Isaiah declared that God would make a highway of holiness for His people, and He would protect them from every danger that would lead them astray or hinder their progress upon it.[27] He would walk with them as a teacher, pointing out the way, and leading them back if they ever wandered.[28] Even the most shortsighted among His people would have no reason for fear, for He would make darkness into light before them and rugged places into plains.[29] Under this new covenant, these words from Proverbs would be fully realized:

> The path of the just is like the shining sun,
> That shines ever brighter unto the perfect day.
> The way of the wicked is like darkness;
> They do not know what makes them stumble (4:18–19).

To the joy of the Christian, all these promises have been fulfilled in Christ, His atoning work on Calvary, and His sending forth of the Spirit. According to the New Testament, God not only predestined a people, but He also prepared beforehand the good works in which they should walk.[30] In the fullness of time, He sent forth His Son to redeem them, and through the preaching of the gospel and the regenerating work of the Spirit, He calls them.[31] All who hear and learn from the Father come to the Son and are granted the right to become the children of God.[32] Because they are sons, God sends forth the Spirit of His Son into their hearts, crying, "Abba! Father!"[33] This same Spirit also seals them, sanctifies them, empowers them, and leads them in the narrow way marked out by Christ.[34] Finally, although they struggle, stagger, and sometimes

---

25. Ezekiel 36:26–27
26. Jeremiah 31:34; 32:39
27. Isaiah 35:8–9
28. Isaiah 30:20–21
29. Isaiah 42:16
30. Romans 8:29–30; Ephesians 1:4–5; 2:10
31. Ezekiel 37:1–14; John 3:3–8; Romans 1:16; Galatians 4:4–5
32. John 1:12; 6:45
33. Galatians 4:6
34. Matthew 7:13–14; Acts 1:8; Romans 8:14; 15:13, 16; Ephesians 1:13, 18–19; 3:16, 20; 4:30; 6:10; Colossians 1:29; 1 Thessalonians 1:5; 2 Thessalonians 2:13; 1 Peter 1:2

fall, the relentless hand of God's providence keeps them until that final day.[35] In this, we see another golden chain of salvation without one broken link. He who began a good work in the life of every believer will perfect it.[36] "What then shall we say to these things? If God is for us, who can be against us?" (Rom. 8:31).

It is not surprising that first-century Christians and their enemies commonly called Christianity "the Way."[37] It is noteworthy that in the book of Acts, Luke refers to it as the *way* of the Lord, the *way* of God, the *way* of truth, and the *way* of righteousness.[38] This is a good reminder for us today, as we are prone to look at Christianity only as a legal position before God based upon faith. Often in our desire to protect the doctrine of *sola fide*, we neglect the truth that Christianity is also a way of life. Jesus Christ is not only our Savior, but He is also our example. We are not only to believe in Him, but we are also to follow Him, imitate Him, and be conformed to Him in thought, word, and deed.[39] For this reason, the apostle John writes, "He who says he abides in Him ought himself also to walk just as He walked" (1 John 2:6).

We must never forget that salvation is by grace alone through faith alone and not of ourselves; it is a gift of God.[40] However, we must also be keen to remember that those who have been saved by grace through faith have become God's workmanship, created in Christ Jesus for good works that God prepared beforehand so that they would walk in them.[41] Those who have believed unto justification have also been regenerated or raised up to walk in newness of life.[42] God has made them to be new creatures with new affections. He has adopted them as children and brought them under His tutelage and discipline.[43] He has made them His workmanship, and He who began a good work will perfect it.[44] For this reason,

---

35. Hebrews 12:5–11
36. Philippians 1:6
37. Acts 9:2; 19:9, 23; 24:14, 22
38. Acts 18:25, 26; 2 Peter 2:2, 21
39. Matthew 16:24; John 10:27; 1 Corinthians 11:1; 1 Thessalonians 1:6: Romans 8:29; 2 Corinthians 10:5; Philippians 3:10
40. Ephesians 2:8–9
41. Ephesians 2:10
42. Romans 6:4
43. Hebrews 12:5–11
44. Philippians 1:6

walking in paths of righteousness is not merely something that Christians ought to do, but it is something that they *will* do.

From our consideration of the Old Testament prophecies and their New Testament fulfillment, we see that a common purpose and ethic will mark all Christians. They will walk in the way that the example and teachings of Christ have marked out for them. Although Christians may be diverse in culture, intellect, maturity—and many other categories— they will possess a striking resemblance in creed and conduct. In fact, the similarities will be so remarkable that only the supernatural work of God can explain them:

- All believe that Jesus Christ is the Son of God, the singular atoning sacrifice for the sins of humanity, and the only name under heaven by which people can be saved.[45]

- All confess with their mouth Jesus as Lord and believe in their hearts that God raised Him from the dead.[46]

- All hold to the Scriptures as the infallible standard for faith and practice and seek to submit their lives to its teaching.[47]

- All strive to keep themselves unstained by the world and pursue sanctification, without which no one will see the Lord.[48]

- All aspire to bear the fruit of the Spirit and to be imitators of God in Christ.[49]

- All seek to love the Lord their God with all their heart, soul, mind, and strength and to love their neighbor as themselves.[50]

- All struggle against sin, mourn over moral failures, confess them to God, and trust in His promises of pardon.[51]

- All are waiting for Christ's return, for they are looking for the city that has foundations, whose architect and builder is God.[52]

---

45. Acts 4:12
46. Romans 10:9
47. John 17:20; 2 Timothy 3:15–17
48. Hebrews 12:14; James 1:27
49. 1 Corinthians 11:1; Galatians 5:22–23; Ephesians 5:1
50. Matthew 22:37–40; Mark 12:30; Luke 10:27
51. Matthew 5:4; Galatians 5:17; 1 John 1:8–10
52. 1 Thessalonians 1:9–10; Hebrews 11:10

This brief list is far from exhaustive, but it is sufficient to demonstrate that God has given His people one heart and one way. Although there are many differences in the church throughout the world, genuine Christians are so united in the essentials of their faith and conduct that the differences are not as significant as they first appear.

The Father has answered Christ's prayer for unity, and the new covenant promises of one heart and one way are a present reality among those who are truly Christian.[53] However, the question remains as to whether we as individuals share in this unity and walk in this narrow way. If a person's beliefs and manner of living contrast with what is true in varying degrees of all genuine Christians, then he should be concerned and question whether he is in the faith.[54]

ONE FEAR

Having considered the church's unity in its affections and essential conduct, we will now turn our attention to a third distinctive of God's new covenant people: a prevailing fear or reverence toward God that leads to wholeness and blessing. Through Jeremiah, God promises, "Then I will give them one heart and one way, that they may fear Me forever, for the good of them and their children after them" (Jer. 32:39).

People often malign and seldom understand the fear of the Lord. However, the Old Testament Scriptures recognize it as the foundation of all virtue and knowledge.[55] It teaches God's people to hate evil and turn away from it.[56] It leads them to love, worship, and serve the Lord with an undivided devotion.[57] It governs human relationship and directs God's people to take great care in their treatment of one another because they know that He will have no part in unrighteousness.[58] For these reasons and many others, the fear of the Lord is held to be a fountain of life and an essential aspect of true godliness.[59] In fact, the fear of the Lord was so central to Old Testament piety that the godly remnant in Israel was often

---

53. Jeremiah 32:38–39
54. 2 Corinthians 13:5
55. Psalm 111:10; Proverbs 1:7; 9:10; 15:33
56. Proverbs 3:7; 8:13; 16:6; 23:17
57. Deuteronomy 6:13; 10:12; 1 Samuel 12:24; 2 Chronicles 19:9
58. Leviticus 25:17; 2 Chronicles 19:7
59. Proverbs 14:27

referred to as "those who fear the Lord" (Mal. 3:16). It is also significant that the prophets said one of the outstanding characteristics of the coming Messiah would be the fear of the Lord:

> The Spirit of the LORD shall rest upon Him,
> The Spirit of wisdom and understanding,
> The Spirit of counsel and might,
> The Spirit of knowledge and of the fear of the LORD.
> His delight is in the fear of the Lord (Isa. 11:2–3).

The word *fear* is translated from a Hebrew word that denotes fear, dread, terror, respect, or reverence.[60] Like many words, especially in the Hebrew language, it has a variety of meanings governed by its context. The enemies of God live in fear of the Lord because of His righteousness and judgments. They know He is a consuming fire,[61] and that it is a terrifying thing "to fall into the hands of the living God" (Heb. 10:31). The mountains melt like wax in His presence, and He dries up the sea with His rebuke.[62] No one can stand in His presence when He is angry, and no one can endure the continual burning of this wrath.[63] For this reason, sinners are terrified, and trembling seizes the godless.[64] They plead with mountains and hills to fall upon them and hide them from the face of God.[65]

In contrast to the wicked, God's people do not live in terror of Him but with a profound and abiding reverence born out of an understanding of the supremacy of His person, the majesty of His attributes, and the perfection of all His works. The glorified saints in heaven clearly reveal this truth in the Song of the Lamb:

> Great and marvelous are Your works,
> Lord God Almighty!
> Just and true are Your ways,
> O King of the saints!
> Who shall not fear You, O Lord, and glorify Your name?
> For You alone are holy.
> For all nations shall come and worship before You,
> For Your judgments have been manifested (Rev. 15:3–4).

---

60. Hebrew: *yir'ah*
61. Exodus 24:17; Deuteronomy 4:24; 9:3; Isaiah 29:6; 30:27, 30; 33:14; Hebrews 12:29
62. Psalm 97:5; Isaiah 50:2; Micah 1:4; Nahum 1:4
63. Psalm 76:7
64. Isaiah 33:14
65. Hosea 10:8; Revelation 6:16

Through the regenerating work of the Holy Spirit, the Christian comes to know something of God's infinite worth, perfect righteousness, indescribable beauty, matchless power, and unfathomable love. This vision, though meager on earth, moves the regenerate heart to reverence God and glorify His name. As the vision grows, so does the believer's reverence. He begins to work out his salvation in fear and trembling because he realizes God is at work in him both to will and work for His good pleasure.[66] He learns to refuse the immorality and impurity that surrounds him, understanding that because of such things the wrath of God comes upon the world.[67] He grows in his ambition to be pleasing to the Lord in all that he does because he knows that he must appear before the judgment seat of Christ and be recompensed for what he has done, whether good or bad.[68] Furthermore, knowing the fear of the Lord, he not only submits his own life to God, but he also strives to persuade others to do the same.[69]

It is also important to note that the fear of the Lord will not only govern the Christian's actions, but it will also have a profound impact upon his relationship with God. It will clothe him in humility. Although the Christian has been granted the privilege to call God his father, he is acutely aware that his Father is in heaven and dwells in unapproachable light as the King of kings and Lord of lords.[70] Although the Christian has access to the Father and is encouraged to come before Him with great boldness, he recognizes that his access is for the sake of Christ, and he does not presume to take any liberty that has not explicitly been granted to him.[71] Finally, although the Christian takes great consolation in the truth that Christ is not ashamed to call him brother, he does not claim equality with Christ or speak of Him except with the greatest admiration and respect.[72] If at any time he discovers that he has in some way trivialized Christ or spoken of Him in an irreverent manner, he is struck in the heart and ashamed.

---

66. Philippians 2:12–13
67. Ephesians 5:3–7
68. 2 Corinthians 5:9–10
69. 2 Corinthians 5:11
70. Matthew 6:9; 1 Timothy 6:15–16
71. Ephesians 2:18; 3:12; Hebrews 4:16. "But the LORD is in His holy temple. Let all the earth keep silence before Him" (Hab. 2:20). "Do not be rash with your mouth, and let not your heart utter anything hastily before God. For God is in heaven, and you on earth; therefore let your words be few" (Eccl. 5:2).
72. Hebrews 2:11

As the Christian grows in his knowledge of the supremacy of God and the greatness of His works, his reverence will increase. In time, it will come to govern every area of his life. Even in the midst of a moral failure, he will find that he possesses a deep and abiding reverence for God from which he cannot escape. This divinely implanted reverence will lead him to repentance and confession.[73]

It is clear that the fear of the Lord is not a common virtue among many professing evangelicals or evangelical churches. Its scarcity is a warning sign that all is not well. Since the fear of the Lord and genuine piety exist in a direct relationship, the diminishing of the one indicates the waning of the other. As we already noted, the fear of the Lord is so foundational to biblical piety that the true people of God were often referred to simply as "those who fear the Lord."[74] We would do well to ask ourselves if those who know us best would describe us in this manner. The decline of the fear of the Lord among God's people is often the result of their ignorance of His attributes and works. The absence of the fear of the Lord is often a sign that the people remain in an unregenerate or unconverted state.

MULTIPLIED BLESSING

Jeremiah 32:38–39 closes with one additional promise regarding the new covenant community: not only would the fear of the Lord and its blessing characterize the individual Christian and the collective church, but these benefits also would overflow into the lives of their children and their children's children. As Jeremiah declares in verse 39, those who fear the Lord do so "for the good of them and their children after them."

The promise of blessing upon the descendants of a man who fears the Lord is common under the old covenant. According to Proverbs, the fear of the Lord not only provides a strong confidence for those who possess it, but it is also a refuge for their children.[75] Genesis 18:19, where God reveals His plan for Abraham, powerfully illustrates the relationship

---

73. In Jeremiah 32:40, God declares, "And I will make an everlasting covenant with them, that I will not turn away from doing them good; but I will put My fear in their hearts so that they will not depart from Me." Although the believer can and should cultivate the fear of the Lord, it is a gift from God that is implanted in the heart at the moment of regeneration.

74. Malachi 3:16

75. Proverbs 14:26

between the godly and their descendants: "For I have known him, in order that he may command his children and his household after him, that they keep the way of the LORD, to do righteousness and justice, that the LORD may bring to Abraham what He has spoken to him."

Because of the patriarch's stewardship of the truth, the God of Abraham was to become the God of Isaac, Jacob, and their descendants after them. Thus, it was the responsibility of each generation in Israel to instruct the succeeding generation by recounting the great redemptive works of God, teaching His commands, and exemplifying true piety through their reverence and obedience. The goal was for each generation to live as a light to its descendants and to the surrounding pagan nations, so that all might be convinced of the benefits of loyalty and obedience to the one true God. It is for this reason that Moses gave the following admonitions to the nation of Israel.

> Hear, O Israel: The LORD our God, the LORD is one! You shall love the LORD your God with all your heart, with all your soul, and with all your strength. And these words which I command you today shall be in your heart. You shall teach them diligently to your children, and shall talk of them when you sit in your house, when you walk by the way, when you lie down, and when you rise up. You shall bind them as a sign on your hand, and they shall be as frontlets between your eyes. You shall write them on the doorposts of your house and on your gates (Deut. 6:4–9).

> Therefore be careful to observe [the commands of God]; for this is your wisdom and your understanding in the sight of the peoples who will hear all these statutes, and say, "Surely this great nation is a wise and understanding people" (Deut. 4:6).

The fathers of each generation were to give themselves wholly to the task of instructing the next. The commands of God were to be upon their heart, and they were to teach them diligently to their sons and daughters. God and His Word were to be the essential part of all life in and out of the home.[76] However, although the Law and the Prophets constantly pressed the seriousness of this endeavor upon Israel, it was rarely obeyed. In fact, the writer of Judges tells us that even the first generation that entered into the Promised Land grossly neglected this stewardship: "When all that

---

76. Deuteronomy 6:6–9

generation [of Joshua] had been gathered to their fathers, another generation arose after them who did not know the LORD nor the work which He
had done for Israel" (2:10).

Although there were brief periods of revival throughout the history
of Israel, they were short-lived. Rarely did one generation fulfill its lofty
calling to teach its children. Rarely did a succeeding generation benefit
from the piety and instruction of the one that preceded it. However, in
this context, Jeremiah prophesied of a future day and covenant in which
every member of God's people would be given a heart to fear the Lord,
not only for his own good but also for the good of his children after him.[77]

We should understand that in these verses God is not guaranteeing the salvation of every child born into a Christian family, but He
is promising that every genuine Christian, every true member of the
church, will be marked by a deep and abiding fear of God that will be
of great spiritual benefit to his children and to all with whom he comes
in contact. In fact, one of the great evidences that a person is truly a
Christian will be the spiritual good that flows from him to those around
him, especially those closest to him, such as a spouse or children. The
same may be said of the collective church. We know that a church is
truly a church because of the spiritual good or benefit that others receive
because of its teaching and piety.

In conclusion, those of us who claim to be Christian must answer
several important questions that remain: Is the fear of the Lord an outstanding characteristic of our lives? Is it an observable reality in our
collective fellowships or churches? Does our reverence for the Lord have
a positive spiritual impact upon those around us, especially upon those
closest to us? Are we faithful in our stewardship to hand down the truth
of God to the succeeding generations? Are we fulfilling our lofty calling
to teach our children, and are they benefiting from our example? It ought
to cause us great concern if these things are foreign to us or rare among
us. They are not options in the Christian faith, but evidences of it.

IMPLICATIONS

We have learned of three vital characteristics of God's new covenant
people: first, those who are truly Christians will possess one heart and

---

77. Jeremiah 32:38–39

unite in their affections for God and for one another. Second, they will possess one way or a singularity of purpose and conduct: they will be followers of Jesus Christ. Third, they will be marked by a genuine fear of the Lord, which will result in their own blessing and the blessing of those after them.

The radical nature of conversion cannot be overstated. Nevertheless, the Christian is not perfected on the day of his conversion. We are all still awaiting our final redemption and ultimate glorification.[78] In spite of all the changes the Holy Spirit has wrought in us, there is an aspect of our fallenness that remains. It sets itself against our new nature and fights against every attempt at conformity to Christ and true piety. The apostle Paul refers to this enemy as our flesh, and he describes the war it wages against us: "For the flesh lusts against the Spirit, and the Spirit against the flesh; and these are contrary to one another, so that you do not do the things that you wish" (Gal. 5:17). The Christian life is a titanic struggle of the new man against the flesh, the world, and the devil, but it is our struggle against sin, our brokenness in the midst of failure, and our pressing on in spite of our wanderings that prove God's work within us.

However, a great disparity exists between what the Scriptures teach about the new covenant people of God and the situation in much of Western evangelicalism. In many cases, humanism and materialism have taken precedent over Godward affections and sacrificial love for the brethren. The core doctrines that were once and for all handed down to the saints have been reinterpreted through the lens of personal preference, Western convenience, and psychology, without the slightest concern for grammar, context, or the creeds and confessions of nobler times. The singular focus of Christlikeness that leads to eternal reward has been replaced with self-realization in the realm of the temporal.[79] The fear of the Lord has been explained away or banished along with all the other biblical doctrines that are considered too harsh for the fragile heart of modern man.

In light of these deviations from Scripture and the most respected confessions of historic Christianity, it is no wonder that the evangelical community seems inundated with carnality and sin. However, the most

---

78. Romans 8:30; 1 Corinthians 15:51–52; Ephesians 1:14; 4:30; Philippians 3:19–20

79. It is important to note that the preoccupation with self-realization requires that God remove Himself from the center of all things and become a servant-god who exists for the promotion of man.

frightening thing about many of the individuals and churches that identify with evangelicalism is not that they struggle against sin, but that they do not struggle at all. The great danger within Western evangelicalism is not that it is tainted with a degree of worldliness, apathy, and self-love, but that it has no problem with the stain. In fact, the great majority do not seem even to notice that it is there. There can be only two possible causes for this blindness to such a terrible and obvious malady.

The first possibility is that many ministers and congregants within evangelicalism are unconverted and carnal. Even in the days of America's Great Awakening, this was the case. The great evangelist George Whitefield (1714–1770) wrote:

> For I am verily persuaded the generality of preachers talk of an unknown and unfelt Christ; and the reason why congregations have been so dead is, because they have had dead men preaching to them. O that the Lord may quicken and revive them, for His own name's sake! For how can dead men beget living children? It is true, indeed, God may convert men by the devil, if He pleases, and so He may by unconverted ministers; but I believe He seldom makes use of either of them for this purpose. No, the Lord will choose vessels made meet by the operation of the blessed Spirit for His sacred use.[80]

Those who suggest that evangelicalism is inundated with the unconverted expose themselves to accusations of lovelessness, self-righteousness, and intolerance. However, we must say it. Even the most adamant confession of faith does not prove a person's conversion. Jesus warned that not everyone who says to Him, "Lord, Lord," would enter the kingdom, but he who does the will of the Father will enter.[81] A Christian is known by his fruits.[82] Therefore, we are not demonstrating love to the many confessing evangelicals who bear no fruit if we let them sleep in Zion while their doom is drawing near. God told the prophet Ezekiel, "Therefore hear a word from My mouth, and give them warning from Me: When I say to the wicked, 'You shall surely die,' and you give him no warning, nor speak to warn the wicked from his wicked way, to save his life, that same wicked man shall die in his iniquity; but his blood I will require at your hand" (Ezek. 3:17–18; see also 33:7–9).

---

80. George Whitefield, *George Whitefield's Journals* (London: Banner of Truth, 1960), 470.
81. Matthew 7:21
82. Matthew 7:16, 20

The second possibility is that many who are genuinely converted languish because of a lack of knowledge, the fault of many who stand in the pulpit. They rarely teach the attributes of God. They either deny or ignore the radical depravity of man. They present the cross as a martyrdom of love rather than a propitiation to satisfy divine justice and appease the wrath of a holy God. They have reduced the gospel to a few statements about Christ that are so sparse in their doctrinal content that they cannot even be considered a creed. They have exchanged the gospel call of repentance and faith for a superstitious transaction made between the sinner and God. Ministers confer assurance of salvation upon those who bow their heads, raise their hand, and repeat a sinner's prayer. Those who profess faith in Christ are rarely challenged to examine themselves to see if they are in the faith or to make their calling and election sure.[83] Very few have heard that without holiness or sanctification no one will see the Lord.[84] Finally, practical principles designed to give people the best possible life in this world have replaced the doctrines that instruct a person in godliness and prepare him for eternity. In spite of all our activity, we have not reduced the famine of the Word of God in the land.[85]

What must we do, then, to bring about a cure? First, we must recognize that the cure is beyond us and cry out to God to have mercy upon the mess that we have made. In the days of Ezekiel, God searched for a man who would build up the wall and stand in the gap before Him so that the people would not be destroyed, but He found no one.[86] By God's grace, may He find us there, night and day, never keeping silent and giving Him no rest until He makes His church a praise in all the earth.[87]

Second, we must be ashamed of all the carnal means we have used to "grow" the church, and we must throw them down with great disgust. We must purge ourselves of Saul's armor and choose only the best stones for our sling: the Word of God, intercessory prayer, and sacrificial love. We must never forget that though we walk in the flesh, we do not war according to the flesh. The weapons of our warfare are not carnal, but divinely powerful for the destruction of every stronghold and obstacle that is set against the gospel and the advancement of Christ's kingdom.

---

83. 2 Corinthians 13:5; 2 Peter 1:10
84. Hebrews 12:14
85. Amos 8:11
86. Ezekiel 22:30
87. Isaiah 62:6–7; See also Ezekiel 36:37–38.

Only in God's power can we destroy the speculations of our age and every lofty thing raised up against the knowledge of God. Only by God's means can we take every thought captive to the obedience of Christ.[88] Third, the need for man's approval must not rule us. We must despise all commendations except those that are proper for a man of God. In this matter, the apostle Paul gives us specific directions:

> But in all things we commend ourselves as ministers of God: in much patience, in tribulations, in needs, in distresses, in stripes, in imprisonments, in tumults, in labors, in sleeplessness, in fastings; by purity, by knowledge, by longsuffering, by kindness, by the Holy Spirit, by sincere love, by the word of truth, by the power of God, by the armor of righteousness on the right hand and on the left, by honor and dishonor, by evil report and good report; as deceivers, and yet true; as unknown, and yet well known; as dying, and behold we live; as chastened, and yet not killed; as sorrowful, yet always rejoicing; as poor, yet making many rich; as having nothing, and yet possessing all things (2 Cor. 6:4–10).

---

88. 2 Corinthians 10:3–5

CHAPTER FIFTEEN

The Everlasting Covenant

---

*And I will make an everlasting covenant with them, that I will not turn
away from doing them good; but I will put My fear in their hearts so that
they will not depart from Me.*

—Jeremiah 32:40

If we are truly Christian, we will soon come to a profound realization
that our security and assurance of salvation rest upon two great columns:
God's covenant faithfulness and His perfect work of redemption on our
behalf.[1] One of the striking and essential characteristics of the genuine
believer is that throughout the full course of his life, he will grow in his
understanding that salvation is all of God, all of grace, and all of Christ.
God loved us, though we did not love Him.[2] He came to our side when
we would not come to His.[3] He made us right with Him when we had no
strength.[4] He will not turn away from us though our failures are numerous and the accusations of conscience and devils overwhelm us.[5]

The mature believer who has grown in his understanding that salvation is all of grace will be deeply troubled by even the slightest suggestion
that his salvation might be the result of his own virtue or merit. He would
rather that his greatest moral failures be exposed and that he be looked
upon with the greatest contempt than for someone to think too much of
him and too little of Christ. Furthermore, he will disdain every accolade
except that which is laid at the feet of Christ. It is for this reason that the

---

1. "For I am the LORD, I do not change; therefore you are not consumed, O sons of Jacob"
(Mal. 3:6). "So when Jesus had received the sour wine, He said, 'It is finished!'" (John 19:30).

2. 1 John 4:10

3. John 3:19–20

4. Romans 5:6

5. 1 John 3:20; Revelation 12:10

mature Christian is not repulsed by the kind of preaching that exposes the universal depravity of man. He knows that the more darkly man is painted, the brighter the Morning Star, Christ, appears.[6]

The mature believer delights in God's work on his behalf and boasts that his justification, sanctification, and ultimate glorification are in Christ alone.[7] The great cry of his heart is, "But God forbid that I should boast except in the cross of our Lord Jesus Christ," and, "Not unto us, O LORD, not unto us, but to Your name give glory" (Gal. 6:14; Ps. 115:1). This truth is set forth with amazing clarity in Paul's letter to the church in Philippi, where he gives us one of the most succinct and yet powerful descriptions of a genuine Christian. He writes, "For we are the circumcision, who worship God in the Spirit, rejoice in Christ Jesus, and have no confidence in the flesh" (Phil. 3:3).

If there is any singular proof of conversion, it is this: the true believer will glory in the person and work of Christ and will not put even the smallest confidence in himself or his deeds. He will reject and disdain every hope of having a righteousness of his own derived from the law, in order that he might be found in Christ, having a righteousness that comes from God on the basis of faith.[8] His great delight and confession will be *sola fide, sola gratia, solus Christus,* and *soli Deo Gloria*!

We cannot exaggerate this truth. As the Christian matures, he will decrease, and Christ will increase.[9] He will abandon all hope in his own merit and trust in the perfect and finished work of another. He will find no confidence in the inward glance, and turn his eyes outward toward Christ alone. A camel loaded with goods cannot pass through the eye of a needle.[10] Neither can a man enter into the kingdom of heaven laden with self-righteousness.

GOD'S COVENANT FAITHFULNESS

Jeremiah 32:40 begins with God's promise to make an everlasting covenant with His people: an immutable and irrevocable pledge that He would never turn away from them to do them good. The term *everlasting*

---

6. 2 Peter 1:19; Revelation 22:16; see also Malachi 4:2; Luke 1:76–79
7. 1 Corinthians 1:30
8. Philippians 3:8–9
9. John 3:30
10. Matthew 19:24; Mark 10:25; Luke 18:25

is translated from a Hebrew word that denotes that which is perpetual, eternal, or unending.[11] This verse employs the term to prove that God's faithfulness to the covenant and the consequences of the covenant would be everlasting.[12] Throughout the years of the believer's life, throughout the many generations left to this present age and in the countless days of eternity to come, the blessings of this new covenant will never expire. The coming of the Messiah has ushered in the last days and is the great fulfillment of all that was prophesied in the Law and the Prophets.[13] The fullness of the times and the summing up of all things in Christ has come upon us.[14] Although we still await the redemption of our bodies and the final consummation of all things, we know that our present standing before God is as perfect as it will ever be.[15] He has become our God, and we are His people. He has "blessed us with every spiritual blessing in the heavenly places in Christ" (Eph. 1:3). Our standing is final, eternal, immutable, and irrevocable. God would sooner break His covenant with day and night and change the fixed patterns of heaven and earth than He would reject His people.[16] Though a woman forget her nursing child and have no compassion on the son of her womb, God will not forget us: He has inscribed us on the palms of His hands.[17]

Although it is not explicitly stated, the specific wording of Jeremiah 32:40 makes it clear that our confidence in the indestructible and immutable nature of the new covenant is to be founded upon the impeccable character of God. Through the prophet Jeremiah, God reveals Himself as the principle actor or prime mover of our salvation and the one upon whom the entirety of the covenant depends. He declares, "I will make an everlasting covenant.... I will not turn away from doing them good; but I will put My fear in their hearts" (Jer. 32:40). Thus, from God's own confession, we learn that the new covenant is based entirely upon His faithfulness and power to accomplish what He has promised. The

---

11. Hebrew: *'olam.*

12. Matthew Henry, *Matthew Henry's Commentary on the Whole Bible* (London: Fleming H. Revell, n.d.), 4:616.

13. Isaiah 2:2; Hosea 3:5; Matthew 5:17; 11:13; Acts 24:14; 28:23; Romans 3:21; Hebrews 1:2; 2 Peter 3:3

14. Ephesians 1:10

15. Romans 8:23; Ephesians 1:14; 4:30; Philippians 3:20–21; 1 Thessalonians 1:10; Revelation 21:1

16. Jeremiah 33:25–26

17. Isaiah 49:14–16

implication of this truth is twofold. First, it brings glory to God. It is His work from beginning to end, and therefore its accomplishment brings glory to Him alone. Second, it is a comfort to His people and serves as the foundation of their strength. Our hearts would melt into despair and be weakened beyond recuperation if even the smallest portion of our salvation was dependent upon us. However, since the covenant is founded upon a God who cannot fail and a work of redemption that is as infinite in duration as it is in value, it is eternal.

At the risk of belaboring the point, we must ask ourselves what hope would even the best of us have if this covenant were anything but unconditional? Even if our worst deeds were culled and we were allowed to present only our finest works before the judgment throne of God, wouldn't such a thought make us tremble? Haven't the Scriptures already testified against us that our most righteous deeds are nothing more than filthy rags? Before God's blazing white righteousness, we would all wither like a leaf, and our iniquities, like the wind, would take us away.[18]

Every Christian who has even the smallest knowledge of the Scriptures will know that our predicament would be terrifying, except for this word given through the prophet Jeremiah, a word as faithful and unfailing as the God who made it. It is a promise as eternal as the divine mind that formed it. It assures us, as believers, that in spite of our inability, we have been brought into an eternal and unconditional covenant with God. It is all of His doing, and, therefore, we have a sure word upon which to stand, not only in this life but also in all the ages to come. It is for this reason that we freely acknowledge with one accord that it is by grace that we are saved, not of ourselves, not of works, lest any among us should boast.[19]

The Old Testament promises regarding the everlasting and unconditional nature of the new covenant are not confined to the prophet Jeremiah but are equally revealed in the words of the prophet Isaiah. Through him, God declared to His people:

> Incline your ear, and come to Me.
> Hear, and your soul shall live;
> And I will make an everlasting covenant with you—
> The sure mercies of David (55:3).

---

18. Isaiah 64:6
19. Ephesians 2:8–9

From this text, we understand that the everlasting covenant that God would make with His people would be founded upon, or according to, the faithful mercies shown to David. Although the phrase is somewhat difficult to interpret, most scholars agree on the following. First, the greatest of all mercies that God showed to David was the promise of the Messiah. Although David would be gathered to his fathers and his lineage would be all but destroyed through sin and rebellion,[20] God promised that a Branch would arise from the fallen tree of David's line.[21] He would restore His people, and through Him, David's house or dynasty would endure forever and his throne would be established without end.[22]

Correspondingly, the eternal covenant that God has made with His people is according to these same faithful mercies. In the fullness of time, when we were without strength and without God in the world, the Messiah came forth from the line of David.[23] He was pierced through for our transgressions, crushed for our iniquities, and by His scourging, we are healed.[24] On the third day, God raised Him up again, putting an end to the agony of death, since it was impossible for Him to be held in its power.[25] Then, He ascended into heaven where He sat down at the right hand of God.[26] Through Him, the fallen tabernacle of David has been rebuilt, so that all humankind may seek the Lord, even the Gentiles who are called by His name.[27] In Him, we have redemption through His blood, the forgiveness of our trespasses, according to the riches of His grace, which He lavished upon us.[28]

---

20. 1 Kings 2:10; Acts 2:29; 13:36. David's dynasty was so reduced by the time of Christ's coming that it could be referred to as "dry ground" (Isa. 53:2) or as a stump of a fallen tree (Isaiah 11:1).

21. Isaiah 4:2; 11:1; Jeremiah 23:5; 33:15; Zechariah 3:8; 6:12

22. "And your house and your kingdom shall be established forever before you. Your throne shall be established forever" (2 Sam. 7:16). "His seed shall endure forever, and his throne as the sun before Me; it shall be established forever like the moon, even like the faithful witness in the sky" (Ps. 89:36–37). "Then to Him was given dominion and glory and a kingdom, that all peoples, nations, and languages should serve Him. His dominion is an everlasting dominion, which shall not pass away, and His kingdom the one which shall not be destroyed" (Dan. 7:14).

23. Romans 1:3; 5:6; Galatians 4:4; Ephesians 2:12

24. Isaiah 53:5

25. Matthew 16:21; John 2:19–21; Acts 2:24; 1 Corinthians 15:4

26. Mark 16:19; Hebrews 1:3; 10:12; 12:2

27. Acts 15:16–17

28. Ephesians 1:7–8

The Messiah came and lifted the ruined house of David when its repair was beyond the power or skill of mortal man. Likewise, He came to us in our ruined and wretched state and made an everlasting covenant with us, not according to our merit, but according to His multifaceted and inexhaustible mercies. Like David, our salvation and its continuance are utterly dependent upon God and His Christ. This truth brings the greatest hope to those who find no hope in themselves. Although our failures are without number, we know that we are secure, because neither God nor His Christ will ever fail in upholding the covenant they have made with us.

Second, the faithful mercies that God showed to David are not limited to his exaltation from shepherd boy to king of Israel or to the promise of an enduring house through the Messiah, but they also refer to the graciousness of God toward David in spite of his unfaithfulness and moral failures. For all of David's virtues, he was still a man with a nature like ours, subject to the flesh, and marred by many trespasses against the law of God.[29] Although he clung to God by faith and never strayed into the idolatrous practices of other kings, several of his recorded sins were notorious. His lie to Ahimelech led to the slaying of the priestly city of Nob.[30] His adulterous relationship with Bathsheba ended in the murder of her husband, Uriah, and the death of David and Bathsheba's infant son.[31] His pride in taking the census resulted in a pestilence that killed seventy thousand men from Dan to Beersheba.[32] Nevertheless, in spite of David's sin, God fulfilled every promise He ever made to him and his house, so that at the end of his days and in his last recorded song, he declares: "Yet He has made with me an everlasting covenant, ordered in all things and secure" (2 Sam. 23:5).

Again, these mercies shown to David and those shown to us in the new covenant are not according to our virtues or merits, but are founded upon the character of our God. The covenant is "ordered in all things and secure," because it rests in Him. He does not change, and therefore we are not consumed.[33] He has promised to do us good, not according to what we deserve, but according to His lovingkindness and tender

---

29. James 5:17
30. 1 Samuel 21:2–10; 22:9–19
31. 2 Samuel 11:2–5, 14–17; 12:15–18
32. 2 Samuel 24:2–17
33. Malachi 3:6

mercies that are ours through faith in Jesus Christ. In fact, it is only in Christ and because of His atonement that the divine mercies that David extolled in his psalms are made possible.

Because of God's everlasting covenant and the promises it contains, the Christian is afforded the greatest security. In Christ, God has made an eternal, immutable, and indestructible covenant with each of us, that He will not turn away from us to do us good. This truth, combined with faith, should give even the most timid saint the greatest hope. It should make the weakest among us as bold as a lion, even when we face the relentless rumblings of conscience and the cruelest slander of the evil one. When the accuser numbers our failures and declares the covenant annulled, we look to the faithfulness of our God and the perfect work of Christ on our behalf. When he comes against us with a vengeance, we cling to Christ with an equal violence. We have no fear and we do not waiver because our hope rests upon the everlasting covenant founded upon the faithful mercies of our God. He will not turn away from us to do us good!

THE BELIEVER'S ADHERENCE

The promises that we have considered so far are the great foundation and source of the believer's hope. Nevertheless, these promises have often been misconstrued: if God has made an everlasting covenant with us so that He will not turn away from us, does it mean that our salvation is secure, even though we live in apathy and rebellion toward His person and will? Are we to continue in sin that grace may increase?[34] Absolutely not! The same God who promised never to turn away from His people also promised to create in them a reverence that would prevent them from ever turning away from Him. Through the prophet Jeremiah, He declared: "And I will make an everlasting covenant with them, that I will not turn away from doing them good; but I will put My fear in their hearts so that they will not depart from Me" (Jer. 32:40).

To properly understand and apply this text, we must recognize that it contains two interdependent promises. Like two sides of a coin, neither can properly exist without the other. In the first promise, God pledges to make an everlasting covenant with His people that He will not turn away

---

34. Romans 6:1

from them, to do them good. However, in the second promise, God pledges to put His fear in the heart of His people so that they will not turn away from Him and fall into a perpetual or fixed state of unbelief and rebellion. Although all stumble in many ways, and some may fall into grievous sin for a season, if they are truly Christian, they will return broken and believing.[35] They cannot ultimately turn away or shrink back to destruction.[36] The greatest confessions of the church reflect this glorious truth:

> And though they [the saints] may, through the temptation of Satan and of the world, the prevalency of corruption remaining in them, and the neglect of means of their preservation, fall into grievous sins, and for a time continue therein, whereby they incur God's displeasure and grieve his Holy Spirit, come to have their graces and comforts impaired, have their hearts hardened, and their consciences wounded, hurt and scandalize others, and bring temporal judgments upon themselves, yet [despite all this] they shall [in time] renew their repentance and be preserved through faith in Christ Jesus to the end.[37]

The conversion of a person is possibly the most magnificent demonstration of the power of God in the universe. Although it necessitates a decision on the part of the individual, it is primarily a work of God from beginning to end. At conversion, God regenerates and transforms a person's heart so that he becomes a new creation.[38] This is not mere poetry, exaggerated metaphor, or hyperbole; it is to be taken literally. Through the regenerating work of the Holy Spirit, a person is given a new nature with new and righteous affections that can no longer tolerate estrangement from God, friendship with the world, or the practice of sin.[39] Although he may stray, he cannot stray for long, but is compelled by many forces within and without to return to God. His new nature will be sickened by his sin and will cause him to loathe it even while the forbidden meat is still between his teeth.[40] The Spirit who indwells him will convict him

---

35. James 3:2

36. Hebrews 10:39

37. Westminster Confession of Faith and the 1689 London Baptist Confession of Faith, chapter 17, "The Perseverance of the Saints." Bracketed notes in part from Peter Masters, pastor of the Metropolitan Tabernacle of London.

38. 2 Corinthians 5:17

39. "Whoever has been born of God does not sin, for His seed remains in him; and he cannot sin, because he has been born of God" (1 John 3:9).

40. Numbers 11:33

of his sin and renew his hope of finding pardon and restoration in the mercies of his God.[41] The Son will seek him out and draw him with great reminders of Calvary's love.[42] The Father will employ every means of providence and stretch forth His hand in loving discipline. He will turn him from the path of destruction, teach him to fear the Lord, and make him a partaker of the very holiness of God.[43] For this reason, the genuine Christian will not turn away or shrink back to destruction. He will persevere unto the end, not only in faith but also in sanctification leading to personal righteousness. The God who began a good work in him will perfect it until the day of Christ Jesus.[44]

It is important to understand that, in the promises of the new covenant, God not only declares what He will do *for* His people, but also what He will do *in* them. The atoning work of Christ *for us* is the foundation of the new covenant and must always have preeminence in our thoughts and devotion. However, the regenerating work of the Holy Spirit *in us* is equally essential. The glory of the new covenant is not only that God will liberate His people from the condemnation of sin, but that He will also free them from its power. The former work is accomplished through the cross. The latter work is accomplished through the regenerating work of the Holy Spirit, who radically transforms or recreates each member of God's new covenant people. As a result, they are not only reconciled to God *legally*, but they bind themselves to Him *devotionally*. Thus, they are truly His people, and He is truly their God.[45]

Here again, we must emphasize that these promises do not negate the reality of the ever-present struggle against sin in the life of even the most mature believer. Nevertheless, to be faithful to the gospel, we must adhere to the truth that "if anyone is in Christ, he is a new creation."[46] He will be inclined toward God, possess a true knowledge of God, and fear God to such a degree that he will not turn away from Him. Although the greatest among us stumble and falter in many ways, even the weakest among us will not turn away from God in a prolonged or settled

41. Isaiah 55:6–13; 57:16–19; John 16:8; Hebrews 4:15–16
42. Luke 19:10; 15:4–7, 8–10; Romans 5:8–10; 1 John 4:9–10
43. Hebrews 12:10 KJV
44. Philippians 1:6
45. Jeremiah 31:33; Ezekiel 36:28
46. 2 Corinthians 5:17

apostasy.[47] We will not because we cannot, and we cannot because we are new creatures who are no longer able to live without the light of God's presence or to endure the darkness and filth of this age.

In light of these truths, it should now be evident that the new covenant promise regarding the believer's adherence to God serves as a litmus test of true conversion. Those who are truly regenerate will persevere or cling to God in hope until the end. Furthermore, they will be marked by a genuine reverence toward God resulting in obedience. In contrast, those who lack such enduring reverence can have little confidence of their part in the covenant. Those who claim to be secure in Christ but do not persevere in faith, sanctification, and the fear of the Lord have little grounds for the hope that is within them. As Bildad the Shuhite declared, "[The hypocrite's] confidence shall be cut off, and [his] trust is a spider's web" (Job 8:14).

The truths of the new covenant serve as a great warning to carnal and apathetic church members who boast of salvation and rest at ease in Zion.[48] They are right in believing that God will never turn away from His people, but they are wrong to presume that they are His people when their lives contradict their confession. They must be solemnly admonished to make their calling and election sure, to examine and test themselves to see if they are in the faith.[49] If there is little evidence of the fear of God in them, then there is little evidence that they have part in the people of God, regardless of the frequency or adamancy of their confession. A biblical assurance that God has made an everlasting covenant with us is possible only to the degree that there is real and abiding proof that He has regenerated our hearts and caused us to reverence Him.

Much of what is practiced within the evangelical community in the West regarding evangelism, conversion, and assurance of salvation is a denial of everything that the Scriptures teach about the new covenant, the new birth, and the very nature of God and salvation. It is for these reasons that the truths found in Jeremiah 32:40 are so important. God has promised never to turn away from those whom He has saved. Yet, He has also promised to put His fear in their hearts so that they will never turn away from Him. We know that we have entered into the new covenant

---

47. James 3:2
48. "Woe to you who are at ease in Zion, and trust in Mount Samaria" (Amos 6:1).
49. 2 Corinthians 13:5; 2 Peter 1:10 KJV

not merely because one time in our lives we prayed a prayer or made a public profession, but because of our enduring and growing reverence for God, which manifests itself in our sanctification. In summary, our sanctification resulting from regeneration is evidence of our justification resulting from faith!

Before we close, it is important to note that this final promise of Jeremiah 32:40 is not only a warning to the carnal church member, but it is also a comfort and encouragement to the true believer when his assurance of salvation is weakened by the condemnation of his heart or the slander of the evil one.[50] The following illustration may help us understand and apply this truth.

Imagine a young man who gives sound evidence of genuine conversion but battles with assurance to the point of despair. Even after frequent and prolonged counseling with several pastors, he finds little reason to hope. The slanderer has beaten him down and magnified his sins to such a degree that he can see little evidence of grace. One day, he pours out his heart to a visiting evangelist. After listening for nearly an hour, the evangelist concludes that the young man has received good counsel on the matter, yet without progress. Therefore, he looks him in the eye and says, "Christ and His gospel appear to have done little for you except to throw you down into a pit of despair and misery. My recommendation is that you simply forget the whole matter and walk away. Abandon Christ and throw yourself headlong into sin. At least by giving full rein to your flesh, you will have joy for a season, and maybe you will become so hardened that you will forget about the future judgment."

The young man is shocked at the evangelist's answer and replies, "I cannot do that."

In quick response, the evangelist asks, "Why not? You have no hope of salvation, and your past struggling against sin has brought you no relief. Why shouldn't you just run from Christ?"

To this the young man cries out, "I cannot run from Christ because salvation is found in Him alone. Though my sin overcomes me a thousand times, I will not run to it because I hate it. I will not turn from God because I fear Him."

At that moment, the evangelist looks in the young man's eyes and simply quotes the words from Jeremiah 32:40: "And I will make an

---

50. 1 John 3:19–20

everlasting covenant with them, that I will not turn away from doing them good; but I will put My fear in their hearts so that they will not depart from Me."

At that moment, the young man's face flushes with astonishment, and he declares, "How could I love Him, unless He has loved me first? How could I hate sin, unless He has renewed my heart? And how could I fear Him, unless He has put His fear within me?" The young man walks away with great assurance and joy in the Holy Spirit.

The power and faithfulness of God both saves and keeps the genuine believer. For this reason, the weakest among us can rest in the fact that God will never turn away from us to do us good. However, to the same degree, we must believe and proclaim that the evidence of true conversion and fellowship in the new covenant is that we will not turn away from God completely nor run headlong into sin as a settled or established practice. The grace of God that is manifest in the new covenant will not lead to apathy or slothfulness in devotion, but rather it will constrain the Christian to greater godliness and spur him on to greater diligence. Of this result we can be sure, not because we trust in the strength of men, but because we understand the purpose and power of God in salvation. He who began a good work in His people will perfect it until the day of Christ Jesus. He has given us new hearts so that we might delight in responding to His person and will.[51] He has given us His Spirit to direct and empower us.[52] He has written His laws upon our hearts and put His fear within us so that we will not turn away from Him.[53] He is our God, and we are His people.[54]

---

51. Ezekiel 36:26
52. Ezekiel 36:27
53. Jeremiah 31:33; 32:40
54. Jeremiah 31:33; 32:38; Ezekiel 36:28

CHAPTER SIXTEEN

God's Goodness to His People

And I will make an everlasting covenant with them, that I will not turn away from doing them good; but I will put My fear in their hearts so that they will not depart from Me. Yes, I will rejoice over them to do them good, and I will assuredly plant them in this land, with all My heart and with all My soul.

—Jeremiah 32:40–42

In this text from the prophet Jeremiah, we have learned three important truths. First, through the atoning work of the Messiah, God has made an everlasting and immutable covenant with His people—He will not turn away from them to do them good. Second, through the regenerating work of the Holy Spirit, He has established His people's disposition toward Him: they will reverence Him and not turn away. Third, having fixed His relationship and disposition toward His people and their relationship and disposition toward Him, He has now cleared the way for the most intimate fellowship and heavenly blessing. All that has stood in the way of God and His people since the fall of Adam has been abolished. Through the redeeming work of Christ, sin has been punished, justice has been satisfied, and a perfect righteousness has been imputed. The regenerating work of the Spirit has removed the hostile heart, broken the power of sin, and given a new heart to the people of God so that they might walk in newness of life.[1] Consequently, God can now rejoice over His people and fulfill the plans He decreed for them even before the foundation of the world—"thoughts of peace and not of evil, to give you a future and a hope" (Jer. 29:11).

---

1. Romans 6:4

DIVINE REJOICING

Periodically throughout the Old Testament Scriptures, God speaks anthropomorphically[2] to describe His sense of burden and grief because of the constant rebellion of His people. At the earliest stages of human history, God declared that He "was sorry that He had made man on the earth, and He was grieved in His heart" (Gen. 6:6). The psalmist informs us that no sooner had God delivered His people from the bondage of Egypt than they "provoked Him in the wilderness, and grieved Him in the desert!" (Ps. 78:40). This is why for forty years He loathed that generation and said they were a people who erred in their heart and did not know His ways.[3] The prophets are even more explicit. Through Ezekiel, God told Israel that He had been hurt by their adulterous hearts, which had turned away from Him, and by their eyes, which had played the harlot after their idols.[4] Through the prophet Isaiah, He bore witness that His people had not called upon Him, but rather they had burdened Him with their sins and wearied Him with their iniquities.[5] In the book of Amos we learn that Israel's corruption and refusal to hear the word of the Lord moved God to declare, "Behold, I am weighed down by you, as a cart full of sheaves is weighed down" (2:13). Finally, the Old Testament comes to a close in Malachi with God's accusation against Israel that they had wearied Him "with [their] words" to the point that He longed for someone "who would shut the doors" of the temple that worship might no longer be offered (Mal. 2:17; 1:10).

God had delivered Israel out of the iron furnace of Egypt and entered into covenant with them at Mount Sinai.[6] He had chosen them to be a people for His own possession out of all the peoples who were on the face of the earth. They were to be a holy nation unto the Lord their God.[7] However, in contrast to their great calling, the overwhelming majority remained unregenerate in heart, hostile to the commands of God, and inclined to every manner of idolatry and immorality. In short, God's

---

2. When God speaks anthropomorphically, He speaks in the manner of a human. For example, God is omnipotent and does not grow weary. However, to accentuate the sins of His people, He may say that their sins have wearied Him.

3. Psalm 95:10

4. Ezekiel 6:9

5. Isaiah 43:22–24

6. Exodus 19:5; Deuteronomy 4:20

7. Deuteronomy 7:6

treasured possession became an unrelenting burden that He was weary of bearing.[8]

It is only in the context of these dreadful accusations against humankind that we can see the power and magnificence of this new covenant promise. Through the atoning work of Christ and the regenerating work of the Holy Spirit, God has now created for Himself a people over whom He can rejoice to do all kinds of good without measure. Because of His work *in us,* He can now be unreservedly *for us.*[9]

Although it is not explained fully in Jeremiah 32:41, the phrase "rejoice over them" denotes the unhindered and unreserved joy of the bridal chamber. This truth is explicit in a similar passage in Isaiah: "And as the bridegroom rejoices over the bride, so shall your God rejoice over you" (62:5). As a bridegroom gives himself willfully, joyfully, and without reservation to his bride, so God gives Himself to His people for their good. There is nothing meager or tightfisted in God's dealings with us. He does not grudgingly give or bless because of some prior commitment on His part that He now regrets. Instead, He gives joyfully—even ecstatically—and without reproach.[10]

The matter should be settled in the believer's heart that God is for him and delights to do him good. However, we must now determine the exact nature of this good that God delights to give us. In light of the teaching of the New Testament, it cannot mean that God rejoices to give us a life of uninterrupted prosperity and ease. Nor can it mean that He is committed to sheltering us from trials, disappointments, or even great suffering. What it does mean is clearly set out for us in Paul's epistle to the church in Rome: "And we know that all things work together for good to those who love God, to those who are the called according to His purpose. For whom He foreknew, He also predestined to be conformed to the image of His Son, that He might be the firstborn among many brethren" (Rom. 8:28–29).

In this text, God has given us both the promise of *good* and an exact definition of what that good is. He has promised to work everything in our lives, from the greatest to the minutest, so that we might be conformed to the image of Christ. Having reconciled us to Himself through the death of His Son, God now rejoices to conform us to His likeness. This is the

---

8. Isaiah 1:14
9. Romans 8:31
10. James 1:5

summum bonum, or greatest good, of the Christian life. It is the highest goal and most extravagant privilege that can be granted to us. All other good things in the Christian life are established upon it and flow from it.

To understand this truth we need only to remember that all of humanity's problems flow from our moral corruption. Our lack of godliness has authored all the maladies of this present fallen age. The promise of our good in this life or in the life to come would be an absolute impossibility apart from our moral transformation to the highest standard possible, which is Christ Himself. A utopia inherited by immoral creatures will soon become a paradise lost. A heaven without Christlikeness would soon become a hell. For this reason, God rejoices over us to conform us to the image of His Son and to bless us with all the good that results from such conformity. We are His workmanship,[11] and He will withhold no good thing from us as He endeavors to transform us from the "rough stock" that we are into the glorious image of His Son, Jesus Christ.[12] As the psalmist declared: "The Lord will give grace and glory; no good thing will He withhold from those who walk uprightly" (84:11).

FAITHFUL PLANTING

To delight or even will to do something is one thing, but to possess the ability or resources to do it is quite another. A poor man may delight to do good to his child and labor at the matter with the greatest strength of will. However, natural limitations may hinder him beyond his control. In the end, all his efforts come to nothing, and his child is disappointed and disillusioned. This is often the case with men, who labor with all their might for the most worthy endeavors and yet fail miserably in all their efforts. However, this is never the case with God. He is the "LORD, the God of all flesh" (Jer. 32:27). He made the heavens and the earth by His great power and outstretched arm. Nothing is too difficult for Him.[13] He works all things after the counsel of His will.[14] His purpose will be established, and He will accomplish all His good pleasure.[15] As the psalmist

---

11. Ephesians 2:10
12. *Rough stock* is stone or wood in its natural state, which has yet to be shaped by the artist's tool.
13. Genesis 18:14; Jeremiah 32:17
14. Ephesians 1:11
15. Isaiah 46:9–10

declares: "The counsel of the LORD stands forever, the plans of His heart to all generations" (33:11).

It is upon the rock-solid foundation of these truths that we interpret God's promise to us in this text: "I will faithfully plant them in this land." God's faithfulness to His exiled people Israel was revealed in the promise that He would gather them from all the lands to which they were dispersed in judgment and bring them into the land that was uniquely set aside as theirs.[16] In the new covenant, this promise is fulfilled in the believer's conformity to Christ and ultimate glorification in heaven. As God was faithful to move entire nations to bring His exiled people home, He is not only faithful, but also powerful to move heaven and earth to conform us to the image of His Son and to bring us home to glory. This was the foundation of Paul's encouragement to the church in Philippi: "Being confident of this very thing, that He who has begun a good work in you will complete it until the day of Jesus Christ" (Phil. 1:6).

The God who governs the universe, who moves the electron around the nucleus, who turns the king's heart wherever He wishes, who both establishes and plucks up entire nations, has set His eye on us for good and will bring us to the place that He ordained for us before the foundation of the world.[17] Unlike the child who is disappointed at the failed promises of a father, we have an infallible hope founded upon better promises.[18] Our God has not only kept His word to free us from the condemnation of sin, but He now also works in us to fulfill His promise to free us from the power of sin. We have His sure guarantee that He is working and will work until the end to conform us to the image of His dear Son. He will see to it that His firstborn Son has a countless congregation of brethren of which He will not be ashamed.[19]

God in Christ is not only the author of our salvation, but also its finisher.[20] Therefore, participation in the process of sanctification is not an option in the Christian life that a believer may or may not choose for himself. It is a certain and indispensable aspect of salvation over which the unfailing providence of God presides. The God who has justified the believer and has given to him His sure promise of future glorification

---

16. Ezekiel 36:24
17. Proverbs 21:1; Jeremiah 18:7–10
18. Hebrews 8:6
19. Romans 8:29; Hebrews 2:11–12
20. Hebrews 2:10; 12:2

will also sanctify him until that final day. Can the one who believes in Christ be certain of justification? Absolutely! Can the one who believes and is justified be certain of glorification? Absolutely! Can the one who believes unto salvation and hopes in future glory be certain that God will continue to sanctify him throughout the full course of his life? Absolutely! As the writer of Hebrews declares:

> If you endure chastening, God deals with you as with sons; for what son is there whom a father does not chasten? *But if you are without chastening, of which all have become partakers, then you are illegitimate and not sons.* Furthermore, we have had human fathers who corrected *us,* and we paid *them* respect. Shall we not much more readily be in subjection to the Father of spirits and live? For they indeed for a few days chastened *us* as seemed *best* to them, but He for *our* profit, that *we* may be partakers of His holiness. Now no chastening seems to be joyful for the present, but painful; nevertheless, afterward it yields the peaceable fruit of righteousness to those who have been trained by it (Heb. 12:7–11, emphasis added).

God will faithfully plant His people in the land and complete the work He has begun in them. His often difficult and yet always purposeful discipline will carry that work out. In fact, one of the greatest evidences of salvation is the reality of God's discipline in our lives, that we might share in His holiness and yield the peaceful fruit of righteousness. To the same degree, one of the greatest evidences of a false faith or empty profession is when a person makes a claim to Christianity, yet God's work of sanctification is absent in his life. He is able to live in sin, be apathetic toward righteousness, and yet remain unscathed by divine discipline.[21] God is not a neglectful father who will allow His children to run wild and unhindered in sin. He not only begets His children, but He also watches over them with the greatest care. He will not withhold His rod from his child, but will demonstrate His love by disciplining him with greatest diligence.[22]

---

21. The word *discipline* is translated from the Greek word *paideúo,* which denotes training, instruction, and chastisement. The word *scourge* is translated from the Greek word *mastigóo,* meaning, "to beat or flog with a whip." The severity of this form of punishment is illustrated in Matthew 10:17, 20:19, and 23:34. Donald Guthrie writes, "Chastisement becomes synonymous with sonship." *The Letter to the Hebrews: An Introduction and Commentary,* Tyndale New Testament Commentaries (Grand Rapids: Eerdmans, 1983), 253.

22. Proverbs 13:24

THE INEXHAUSTIBLE RESOURCES OF DEITY

The true believer's noticeable progress in sanctification is not the result of his strength of will or degree of dedication. It is not something he adds to his faith in order to be saved, but rather it is the result of his faith. The God who justified him has also regenerated him and made him into a new creature with new affections and a new power to live a Godward and godly life. As the apostle Peter writes, "His divine power has given to us all things that pertain to life and godliness" (2 Peter 1:3).

In Jeremiah 32:40–42, we find one of the most amazing promises in all of Scripture. In fact, it is an expression found here and nowhere else. Through the prophet Jeremiah, God promises to work for our sanctification with *all His heart and with all His soul.*[23] This anthropomorphic statement does not teach that there are physiological similarities between God and man, but only that He will draw upon the inexhaustible resources of His deity to carry out His purposes in His people. It tells us that our sanctification and ultimate glorification are not trivial matters for God, but are of such importance that He promises to employ the very fullness of His deity in order to ensure their accomplishment! It is astounding that God both created and sustains the universe with a word, and yet He has promised to work for the believer's sanctification and ultimate glorification with the entirety of His person and power.[24]

This amazing statement has a twofold application as a promise instilling hope and as a warning evoking fear. For the believer it is a promise. Even the strongest among us struggles with sin and its accompanying discouragements. We are in constant need of seeing the finish line at the end of the race and of being assured that we will reach the end victoriously. We need something greater than a "little engine that could" mentality. We need a confidence far beyond our determination and stamina. We need the aid of one greater than us, whose strength is as infinite as His mercy and whose character is of the highest quality. We need a God who "works all things according to the counsel of His will" and perfects every work He has begun.[25] It is therefore the greatest encouragement to know that the Author and Finisher of our faith has pledged Himself entirely to the accomplishment of our salvation. Although the speed and degree

---

23. Jeremiah 32:41
24. Genesis 1:3–31; Hebrews 1:3; 11:3
25. Ephesians 1:11; Philippians 1:6

of progress in the faith will vary from believer to believer, and although some will run to the mountaintops and others will walk only in lower regions, all will grow, all will make noticeable progress in the faith, all will be conformed in gradual degrees to the image of Jesus Christ.

Correspondingly, this text is also a great warning to those who do not progress in the faith, but stagnate in their profession; who hold to a form of godliness, but deny its power; who call upon the name of the Lord, but are without inward devotion, genuine piety, and the pursuit of holiness, without which no one will see the Lord.[26] It is a warning to all that a tree is known by its fruit, and the evidence of justification is the ongoing work of sanctification. God has pledged Himself entirely to the believer's sanctification and ultimate glorification. Therefore, those who profess Christ and yet demonstrate little or no evidence of the transforming work of divine providence are building their house on sand:[27]

> So are the paths of all who forget God;
> And the hope of the hypocrite shall perish,
> Whose confidence shall be cut off,
> And whose trust is a spider's web.
> He leans on his house, but it does not stand.
> He holds it fast, but it does not endure (Job 8:13–15).

Let the struggling believer be comforted; let the apathetic church member be warned. The great evidence of true conversion is God's ongoing work of sanctification in our lives. If we have been saved by grace through faith, we are now God's "workmanship, created in Christ Jesus for good works, which God prepared beforehand so that we should walk in them" (Eph. 2:8–10). The evidence that God has begun a good work in us is that He continues that work until that final day.[28]

---

26. 2 Timothy 3:5; Hebrews 12:14
27. Matthew 7:26
28. Philippians 1:6